Extraordinary Women
from U.S. History

Extraordinary Women from U.S. History

Readers Theatre for Grades 4-8

Chari R. Smith

TEACHER IDEAS PRESS
Portsmouth, NH

Teacher Ideas Press
A division of Reed Elsevier Inc.
361 Hanover Street
Portsmouth, NH 03801-3912
www.teacherideaspress.com

Offices and agents throughout the world

The author and publisher wish to thank those who have generously given permission to reprint borrowed material:

Introduction adapted by permission from *Readers Theatre for Beginning Readers* by Suzanne I. Barchers. Published by Teacher Ideas Press (1993).

Excerpts from *Eleanor Roosevelt's My Day, Volumes 1–3* edited by David Elmblidge. Published by Pharos Books (1989, 1990, 1991). Reprinted by permission from Nancy Roosevelt Ireland.

Library of Congress Cataloging-in-Publication Data

Smith, Chari R.
    Extraordinary women from U.S. history: readers theatre for grades 4–8 / by Chari R. Smith.
       p. cm.
    Includes bibliographical references.
    ISBN: 1-56308-989-0
    1. Women—United States—Juvenile drama. 2. Children's plays, American. I. Title.
    PS3619.M555 E35 2003
    812.008'352042—dc21
                                                                                    2003013595

Editor: Suzanne Barchers
Production coordinator: Angie Laughlin
Typesetter: Westchester Book Services
Cover design: Joni Doherty
Manufacturing: Steve Bernier

Printed in the United States of America on acid-free paper

07 06 05 04 03 ML 1 2 3 4 5

*This book is dedicated to a special group of extraordinary women
from the Happy Hour Group,
Alice, Ellie (my Mom), Karen L., Karen T., Marge, and Sue*

Contents

Acknowledgments

I would like to take the opportunity to thank the many people who have contributed to the development of this book. Suzanne Barchers has been a tremendous support and inspiration for this book. I very much have appreciated her encouragement and guidance.

This book required extensive research. Without the help of Multnomah County Library in Portland, Oregon, this book would have been impossible to complete. Thanks to their helpful librarians, incredible system, and plentiful books on all of the women.

Grace Ruth at San Francisco Library, SCBWI members Carol Peterson, Pamela Turner, Keely Parrack, and Nancy Case for their support. Sarah Smith at Camp Fire USA for her willingness to review the scripts. Gigi Lirot for her flying expertise and telling me what a yolk is for *Earhart Takes Flight*.

Many teachers were a part of testing out the scripts in their classrooms. Special thanks to those teachers: Jody Rutherford from Kellogg Middle School in Portland, Oregon; Jennifer Thelen from Irvington Elementary School in Portland, Oregon; Melissa Coviello at an elementary school Park City, Utah; and Shannon Brooks from Eleanor Roosevelt Elementary School.

In the development of the play about Sacagawea, I discovered many discrepancies on the actual events of her life. Special thanks to the following people who are experts in the Lewis and Clark expedition and provided insight and guidance in the composition of this play: Pat Nida, Robey Clark and Larry McClure from the Northwest Regional Educational Laboratory and Jay Rasmussen from the Lewis and Clark Trail Heritage Foundation.

In the development of the play *Eleanor*, Eleanor Roosevelt's granddaughter, Nancy Ireland Roosevelt, was kind to give me permission to use quotes from Eleanor Roosevelt's newspaper column "My Day."

My colleague and friend Theresea Deussen and her family—Boerge Klevang Pedersen, Aaron Shirzadegan, and Anoush Shirzadegan—for listening to my ideas, trying out the plays with her family, and being of great support.

Karen Romeo introduced me to teaching the arts in Boulder, Colorado. Every theatrical pursuit stems from her support and guidance during those formative times.

My husband, Tom, puts the "extra" in this extraordinary life we share. I am grateful to him for supporting my creative endeavors.

Introduction

"Readers theatre is a presentation by two or more participants who read from scripts and interpret a literary work in such a way that the audience imaginatively sense characterization, setting, and action. Voice and body tension rather than movement are involved, thus eliminating the need for the many practice sessions that timing and action techniques require in the presentation of a play" (Laughlin and Latrobe, 1990, 3).

Traditionally, the primary focus of readers theatre is on an effective reading of the script, not on a dramatic more memorized presentation. Generally, there are minimal props and movement on the stage.

The scripts in this collection were developed from historical events. Elements have been added for the purpose of illustrating the time period in which the women lived. Some of the characters are fictitious and represent people these famous women were likely to have met.

Students are not expected to memorize lines in readers theatre. Instead, they read from the scripts during the presentation. The focus is on learning about the historical events of the women's lives and bringing those events to life in the classroom. Although students are not creating a dramatic production of the script, the nature of the presentation encourages the development of important skills. The students who read are building their oral presentation skills while the students in the audience build their listening skills.

Students are able to explore historical events through a new medium and gain an appreciation for the experiences these women endured. Readers theatre is easy to prepare, thus making it a perfect choice for presenting to parents and other classes for special days when a program is expected.

GETTING STARTED

For the first read through, a script takes approximately 30–45 minutes to complete. With rehearsals, a script may take 20 minutes. Once you have chosen which script to present, make enough copies for everyone in your class. Next, assign the parts to those students who volunteer. There is no need to have formal auditions for the characters. Students should then read through the script on their own and may highlight their lines. This preparation will allow them to become familiar with the script. You can also choose to do two scripts at the same time and divide the students into two groups. Each group can then present their script to the other group.

For the presentation, you will need to make sure you have a large enough space. If your classroom doesn't have a large open area, you may want to consider reserving a larger space for that time period. Having enough space for the presenters to stand and for the audience to sit is an important consideration to have a successful presentation.

The preparation time is minimal and allows the scripts to be easily incorporated into your lesson plans. The chapters are organized into sections. These sections include background, presentation suggestions, list of characters, props, the script, and follow-up activities.

Background

Each chapter contains a background. This provides an easy reference for you when determining which script is best appropriate for your lesson plans. This summary provides basic information about the woman's life depicted in the script, as well as other pertinent facts about her.

Presentation Suggestions

Presentation Suggestions follows the Background information. Generally, there are a few presentation suggestions for each play. Recommendations for staging and backdrops may be included in this section.

For the staging in readers theatre, readers traditionally stand—or sit on stools, chairs, or the floor—in a formal presentation style. The narrators may stand with the script placed on a music stand slightly off to one side, with one on each side.

The position of the reader indicates the importance of the role. For example, in *Harriet's Road to Freedom,* Harriet should be positioned front and center through most of the reading. When there are several characters that have brief parts, the characters may enter for their reading and then leave the stage. You may also choose to simply have all students sit in a circle and read through the script. Students may also have additional ideas on arrangements. Their suggestions should be encouraged to include them in the process of creating a presentation.

If you choose a script to present for parents or another class, you may want to consider creating a simple backdrop. This is easily accomplished by using large cardboard boxes. Students can draw, paint, or use another medium to create a backdrop. A simple backdrop may be a field and sky setting the tone for the presentation or a mural depicting the life the woman lived. You may also want to consider collaborating with the art teacher if you are preparing a formal presentation. Students can create the backdrop in art class with the guidance of the art teacher.

Props

Props are used sparingly in readers theatre. Each chapter contains a list of props that are optional for each script. Props may include a handkerchief, purse, or a book. Anything hand-held is considered a prop.

If you choose to use props, you may also want to consider assigning a student to be propmaster. The propmaster would be responsible for handing the reader the necessary prop that the script calls for. The props may be kept in a box off to one side of the stage and the propmaster would then deliver the prop to the character that needs it.

List of Characters

Each script has a varying number of parts. Each script has two narrators, but if you have a large class, you may divide the narrator role into three or four parts. If the number of characters in a script is greater than the number of students in your class, assign students multiple parts.

Most of the scripts have two to three parts that are flexible. For example, in *Anthony's Fight for Women's Rights* the list of characters calls for "women at the registrar's office." This may mean one student or five students play this role.

Follow-up Activities

These activities are designed for further exploration of the women's life. They may include research projects, writing assignments and/or improvisational theatre games discussed in Chapter Two. You may choose to use improvisational theatre to further explore the time period discussed. Improvisational theatre is an excellent tool to encourage creativity, build teamwork, and develop oral presentation skills.

CONCLUSION

The chapters are designed to make it easy for you to use readers theatre in your classroom. These scripts may be used several times. You may also consider preparing these presentations for assemblies, parent's day, or other performance opportunities.

Once students have presented the scripts, they may choose to develop the script further into a production. This activity offers students the opportunity to work together to create a dramatic production. They may choose to eliminate the narrators and implement stage direction, as well as additional characters.

They also may choose another event in the woman's life and create their own play about that portion of the person's life. For example, *Eleanor* depicts the early portion of Eleanor Roosevelt's life. Students may create a script based on the latter part of Eleanor's life when she was the first lady, or on other events that occurred during her lifetime.

REFERENCE

Laughlin, Mildred Knight, and Kathy Howard Latrobe. *Readers Theatre for Children: Scripts and Script Development*. Englewood, CO: Teacher Ideas Press, 1990.

Chapter One

Warm-up Theatre Activities

THE FUNDAMENTALS OF ACTING

This section provides a starting point for those who have never used theatre in the classroom to the experienced theatre teacher. It provides the foundation for doing the readers theatre scripts, improvisational theatre activities, and any other theatrical elements you wish to incorporate into your curriculum.

Acting is creating the illusion that you are someone other than yourself. Actors achieve this illusion by transforming themselves into characters. Some of the best actors are able to convince an audience of their characters by changing everything about themselves. Their voice, mannerisms, body language, walk, and body shape—all or only one may change to become the character. Others hardly have to change at all, because they are "typecast" into roles, which means the characters they are playing are similar to themselves.

Teaching acting to young children should not be approached as producing another Hollywood star. Begin with the basic acting skills; teach young children how to change their voices, facial expressions, and walks to become different characters. Changing the voice, walk, and facial expression are easy qualities for a child to understand and relate to basic characters (e.g., how an old person speaks versus a baby). These should be reviewed every time you begin a theatre game or play.

In readers theatre, there is little movement; therefore, changing the walk is not utilized as frequently in these scripts. However, in improvisational theatre activities it is used and therefore should be explored.

Voice

The best way to teach your students about changing their voices is to give them examples. Using the phrase "I love acting," call on different students to change their voices to sound like the following characters:

baby

monster

shy person

very old person

Using the phrase "I love acting" for the four different characters should illustrate to your students how changing your voice can change whom you sound like. Ask students what changed about the voice with each character. Answers should be pitch (a high voice or a low deep voice) and dynamics (how loud or soft the voice was). Do some characters wrong; for example, talk to students like a baby and ask them if you sound like a very old person. Of course, the answer is you do not. Showing the difference between the right way to change your voice to match a character and the wrong way clearly defines how changing the voice is an important part of acting.

Facial Expression

The face has many features that can be changed. The eyes, nose, and mouth can be widened or scrunched up, depending on the character. Read the following list of emotions to students. With students sitting, ask them to put on the face of each emotion. You might ask, "What does this emotion look like on your face?" Have them hold that emotion for about three seconds, then move on to the next one.

angry

mean

disgusted

sad

happy

scared

hurt

surprised

Walk

In acting, how you walk can let an audience know a lot about a character. Clear the room and have all the students stand on one side of the room, shoulder to shoulder. There should be enough room for them to walk across to the other side. Before beginning this exercise, show them an example of bad acting. Walk across the room briskly with a straight back and ask them if that is how a really old person would walk. Of course the answer is no, it is not how a really old person would walk. Ask them to tell you what you could do to convince them you are a really old person. Answers are walk slowly, bend your back, pretend you have a cane, and so on.

Call out the following emotions and types of characters and have students cross the room like those characters or persons with those emotions. For example, if you call out a sad person, they all cross the room in the way they believe someone sad would walk. Remind students that this is a game for how characters walk, not run. Instruct them to stop when they get to the other side of the room. When they have all crossed as sad persons, they wait for the next emotion or character and cross back. Use the example of an old person before they try it. Try some or all of the following characters and emotions:

very old person

baby

sad

happy

scared

monster who walks slowly

spy (quiet and calculating)

nervous

superstar model or famous person

Encourage students who are having difficulty and compliment those who are doing a good job. Again, remind students this is not a running exercise, and each character should cross the room.

If there are more emotions or characters for the walks, faces, and voices you would like to use, feel free to add them to the list. Again, review the three changes—voice, walk, and facial expression—before doing any theatre activities or plays. It is important to continue to develop these skills in students so they can use them in plays and future theatre experiences.

IMPROVISATIONAL THEATRE

Improvisational theatre is an excellent way to warm up students before doing a readers theatre script. These activities have been passed on from person to person, teacher to teacher, for decades. I have learned improvisational theatre through studying with several teachers and am pleased to pass on these valuable activities from them to you. There are literally hundreds of variations of each theatre exercise, all geared to develop acting skills.

Improvisational theatre offers a vehicle to develop more than just acting skills. Students build self-esteem, confidence, and teamwork skills and have fun overall. Theatre games can be divided into two categories: movement and interactive. Movement games generally do not include any dialogue, but instead focus on warming up the body and building teamwork. Interactive games develop scenes and plots and delve deeper into character development.

Movement Activities

Game: Machine

Duration: 10–15 minutes

Preparation: Create a space as a stage

The Machine is a timeless icebreaker when introducing students to theatre. To begin, ask the students questions:

What is a machine?

What are examples of machines in your house? (TV, washer, dryer, microwave, etc.)

What makes a machine work? (screws, buttons, nails, electric parts, etc.)

What does a machine sound like? (Ask for examples of sounds like "squeak," "bop," and other sounds students make to imitate a machine sound.)

"What we're going to do today is make a machine, and all of you will be the parts."
Ask a student to volunteer to come on "stage."
"Each of you will be a part of the machine by working together. Now (to the student on stage) choose a machine movement to make. You can move your arms up and down. Wiggle your hips side to side. Remember to do something that you can repeat for the next several minutes."
Choose another student to come on stage to add to the machine.
"Find somewhere to add to the machine. You can be on the floor moving your arms in front of his/her legs. You can stand behind the machine part moving your arms over his/her head.

However you add to the machine, be sure you are somehow a part of it. Don't just stand next to someone doing your own movement. Figure out how to be parts of a machine, working together."

Ask another student to come onstage. Continue having students come on stage until your entire class is a machine. Everyone should be making his or her own machine noise. You should stand at one end of the machine where everyone can see you.

"I am at the controls of the machine and I am slowing it down (everyone should slow down together, including the sounds). Now I am speeding up the machine."

Continue slowing and speeding up the machine as you see fit. At the end of the exercise, turn the machine off and all students should completely stop.

This activity works best as a warm up before doing additional theater games or a readers theatre script.

Game: Mirror

Duration: 5–15 minutes

Preparation: No stage is needed, just enough space for students to move around.

The Mirror Game is a great activity for students to become more focused. Students work with a partner. Once all students have chosen a partner, select a volunteer to demonstrate this game.

"The idea behind the mirror game is to move as if you are the reflection of your partner. So today, Kelsey will be my reflection. We'll start with our hands raised toward each other. There's an invisible wall between us, so we can't touch each other. I will slowly move my right hand up, and Kelsey will move her left hand up to mirror my movement. There's also no talking during this game. I can't tell her what I'm going to do, she has to follow."

"You also don't want to try to trick your partner and move too fast (move fast to demonstrate) or move your legs and other body parts. We're going to start with just our arms and hands."

Ask Kelsey to go back to her partner.

"When I say switch, without putting down your hands the other person will lead. So start standing and facing your partner. Decide who is going to lead first and begin."

At this point, you just want to walk around and make sure students are working slowly, trying to mirror their partner. Occasionally, students will talk. Remind them this is a no-talking exercise. Concentration is key. In some cases, students will forget who is leading and who is mirroring. When they have reached that point, they have really connected with their partner. After a minute or two, announce switch.

For more advanced students, have them switch the leader position at least twice. Then instruct leaders to slowly sit down while their partners mirror them. The advanced version of this activity includes students moving more than just their hands and arms. They can move their legs, feet, shoulders, anything as long as the intent of the activity remains intact.

Game: Sculptures

Duration: 10–20 minutes

Preparation: No stage is needed for this game, but space is needed for students to move around.

This activity works well right after engaging in the Mirror Game. Students will need a partner for Sculptures, and because the Mirror Game also uses partners, it's a perfect segue.

To begin, ask students, "What is a sculpture?" Usually students answer this question with "Something that stands still." Then ask, "What can it be made out of?" The answers to this question are endless. Some examples include ice, bronze, metal, wood, and many more. The answer you are waiting for is clay.

Ask for a volunteer from the audience to demonstrate this exercise. Have the student start as a lump of clay, head down.

"This is a lump of clay. I'm going to make an angry sculpture. I move the arms and legs into what I think angry looks like."

Move the student into an angry sculpture as if he/she was clay.

"Notice, I am not moving parts that won't stay still by themselves. For example, if I move her ear, will it stay there? No. So, only move what will stay still by itself. When you are done with your sculpture, stand back so I know you are done."

Students engage in the Sculpture Game with partners. The first step for them is to decide who will be clay first, and who will be the sculptor. Instruct students to make an angry sculpture. When they are done, have them switch. Now, whoever was clay is now the sculptor and vice versa.

Other emotions to create sculptures of include sad, happy, and scared. You may also choose for them to make characters such as a monster, a lion, and other characters.

Interactive Activities

Interactive activities use voice, facial expression, and walk. They encourage creativity and teamwork. Students have the opportunity to apply their budding acting skills in activities such as the Chair Game and Situation Improv. Because these activities may go on for 10 minutes or an hour, there is no suggested duration time designated.

Game: Chair

Duration: Indefinite

Preparation: Set a chair on the designated stage space

The Chair Game is one of the first improvisational theatre games I was taught, and it's extremely popular across all age groups. I would suggest reviewing why the voice, facial expression, and walk should be changed when acting. This exercise is the perfect opportunity for students to hone those fundamentals of acting.

Introducing this game to students may include the following instructions:

"In this game, you have to become a character that needs this chair. There are some rules, whoever is sitting in the chair has to go along with whoever comes on stage. So, if I come on stage and say there's wet paint on the chair, the person in the chair can't argue with me.

The chair can be anywhere—on a spaceship, in a doctor's office, in a car. You can be anywhere—the jungle, a movie set, or in school. The key is to come up with a character that has to have this chair. Anything can be on the chair too.

Let's do an example. I'll start offstage."

At this point, start about ten steps from the chair as if you were walking across the stage. Casually stroll across the stage and announce you are a ninety-year-old woman and you need to sit down. Ask your students, "Do you believe me?"

The answer would be no. This is the opportunity to review the fundamentals of acting. If you're going to act like an old woman, your walk, voice, and facial expression would need to change to be convincing.

Another rule in the Chair Game is that there are no repeats. Once a reason is given it cannot be used again. There's also no touching in this game, so the person coming on stage cannot touch the person in the chair or the chair itself.

This game can continue indefinitely. One student comes on stage, gets the person out of the chair. Then that student sits in the chair. The next student gets that student out of the chair, and so on. I would suggest playing this game long enough for everyone to have one turn.

Reasons for someone to get out of the chair may include:

"The doctor is ready to see you in the office now. Sorry to keep you waiting."

"Don't sit there, I just painted that chair!"

"How did you get onto my throne? Guards!"

"Um, that is the director's chair and I'll get in BIG trouble if he catches you there. I'm the assistant. So if you could please go before he comes here and starts yelling, I would appreciate it."

The Chair Game offers endless possibilities for students to become different characters.

Situation Improv

There are many variations of Situation Improvs. The most common version is Freeze. Two students begin on stage. They improvise a scene and become two characters trying to solve a problem.

For example, one student may say, "I can't believe I got another flat tire!"

The other student reacts to this statement and assumes they are stuck somewhere trying to fix a flat tire. The idea of this game is to create a situation, with no script. The goal is to encourage creativity. At some point, you would say freeze, and the two students on stage would freeze.

A third student would come on stage and replace one of the two students. This new person would take the exact physical position of one of the students. For example, if one student was kneeling down to check the flat tire, the new person would take this exact position.

The new person would then start an entirely new scene using the position. It is important to emphasize to students to use the position as a part of the scene.

In this instance, the new person may start the scene by saying, "I don't know where your contact lens is, I can't find it."

Or, "This is pointless, we'll never find the buried treasure using our hands."

Notice how both of these lines gave important information to the other person on stage. The first line in Freeze communicates to the other person on stage where they are and allows them to react appropriately. Before beginning the game, it may be useful to have all students write down three situations they may use in Freeze. This will help get the "creative juices" going.

Eventually, you may choose to have students shout freeze. If you do, be aware that some students may shout freeze too quickly, not allowing scenes to develop. And make sure other scenes don't go on too long. If no one is shouting freeze, you should.

Another situation improv is for students to create a scene from beginning to end on the spot. The audience decides where and who the two characters on stage are. For example, the audience may decide they are at the circus. The Lion has stage fright, and the M.C. is trying to convince him to go on stage.

This type of Situation Improv allows students to develop the plot for a scene, with a beginning, middle and end. Explain to students they are to solve the problem in the scene. When asking the audience for suggestions, start with the following:

Where are they? (doctor's office, another planet, garbage truck, and so on)

Who are they? (It does not always have to relate to where they are)

What is the problem they are trying to solve?

Situation Improvs are excellent resources for students to hone their acting abilities, build teamwork, and have fun.

CONCLUSION

The fundamentals of acting—voice, facial expression, and walk—are great to review before engaging in theatre activities. Improvisational theatre may be a warm-up exercise before doing a script, used as follow-up activities after presenting a script, or performed as a separate activity. Students enjoy the opportunity to be creative. Both interactive and movement improvisational activities develop basic acting skills. Students immerse themselves into several different characters and situations. Through theatre, students may build teamwork and self-confidence, and have fun!

REFERENCE

Greenberg, Chari. *Little Plays for Little People*. Englewood, CO: Libraries Unlimited/ Teacher Ideas Press, 1996.

Chapter Two

Sacagawea
(1787–1812)

Sacagawea and Her Journey West

BACKGROUND

Sacagawea was a Shoshone woman who traveled with the well-known Lewis and Clark expedition in the early 1800s. Although many stories would have us believe she was hired as a guide, she was not. Sacagawea was the wife of French-Canadian fur trader Toussaint Charbonneau. He was hired as an interpreter for the journey. Sacagawea and their two-month-old son, Pomp, accompanied them.

In reality, Sacagawea proved to be an invaluable part of their team. She knew how to communicate with the Lemhi Shoshone, recognize geographic landmarks, and harvest the lands for food; she also saved precious cargo from sinking in the waters and convinced her Shoshone brother to trade with the men of the Lewis and Clark expedition for their horses so they could cross the mountains. Although she was not paid for her services, her contribution to the expedition undeniably led to its success. As the only Native American woman with a baby on the expedition, she was a visible sign of peace.

This play depicts the portion of her life when she met Lewis and Clark and traveled with the Corps of Discovery to their encounter with the Shoshone tribe (1804–1805).

Please note, a great deal of controversy lies around the actual historical events that occurred. This play is based on several resources and depicts one of many versions of what is believed to have happened.

PRESENTATION SUGGESTIONS

The narrators should remain on either side of the stage. Sacagawea may want to have Pomp on her back before starting the presentation. Characters should enter and stand center stage. This play may be best presented first reading in a circle, with no movement at all. Students may then collectively decide how to stand during the presentation.

For a backdrop, consider having students create a mural depicting the route Sacagawea traveled with the Lewis and Clark expedition. The mural may be decorated with the variety of plants discovered, animals in different regions, and streams and rivers that run through the region of land. The mural may also have petroglyphs/Indian art representing people who have lived in this country for centuries.

PROPS (OPTIONAL)

1. Baby in a blanket to be Pomp[1]
2. Two mugs, for the drinks York serves

3. American flag
4. Fiddle

LIST OF CHARACTERS

1. Narrator 1
2. Narrator 2
3. Sacagawea (suk-kah-guh-WEE-ah)
4. Hidatsa woman
5. Toussaint Charbonneau (too–SAHNT SHAR-buh-noh)
6. Captain Meriwether Lewis
7. Captain William Clark
8. York, *Clark's servant*
9. George Drouillard (Drewyer), *an interpreter*
10. Private Joseph Field
11. Private Robert Frazier
12. Private Pierre Cruzette
13. Private Hugh McNeal
14. Private John Shields
15. Private William Bratton
16. Chief Cameahwait (kah-MEE-ah-wayt), *leader of Shoshone tribe*
17. Shoshone girl

Optional:

Soldiers from Corps of Discovery

Shoshone warriors

‖ Sacagawea and Her Journey West ‖

Scene One
Setting: In the fields.

> **Narrator 1:** Sacagawea was born in the late 1700s in the Lemhi Shoshone tribe, near the Rocky Mountains. When she was about eleven years old, Hidatsas captured her and took her far from her home.

> **Narrator 2:** As a teenager, she was purchased by Toussaint Charbonneau. He was a French-Canadian fur trader who already had another wife. She lived with him among the Hidatsa and Mandan tribes.

> **Narrator 1:** Our story begins in the fall of 1804. Charbonneau's two wives harvested corn in the fields together while they talked.

> **Hidatsa woman:** Have you seen the fort the strangers have built? They have medicines, cloth, and many other fine items.

> **Sacagawea:** No, I have not. Although, Charbonneau speaks of it frequently. They plan to travel west, over the mountains.

> **Hidatsa woman:** Do they know the land there?

> **Sacagawea:** No, I believe that is why they are going. To learn about the land beyond the one they know.

> **Narrator 2:** Sacagawea stretched her back and drew in a deep breath.

> **Hidatsa woman:** How are you feeling?

> **Sacagawea:** I suppose as well as can be expected. I don't know if we'll have a boy or a girl.

> **Hidatsa woman:** I guess a boy.

> **Sacagawea:** We shall see, soon.

Scene Two
Setting: Fort Mandan.

> **Narrator 1:** Charbonneau was invited to meet with Captains Meriwether Lewis and William Clark at Fort Mandan.

> **Narrator 2:** Sacagawea, Charbonneau, Drewyer, Captains Lewis and Clark sat around a fire talking. York stood near where Clark sat.

> **Lewis:** We were sent by President Thomas Jefferson to learn about the land that lies west.

Clark: We don't know the people we will encounter in our journey. We need help understanding their languages, customs, so we can pass in peace.

Charbonneau: I see.

Clark: York, please bring drinks for our guests.

York: Yes sir.

Drewyer: I am George Drouillard. Most call me Drewyer. My role is to be the interpreter. I know some languages, but I am not familiar with the people who are farther west. What languages do you know?

Charbonneau: I can speak some Shoshone because of one of my wives, Sacagawea. Her tribe is far west, and you will be in need of my services to pass safely.

Narrator 2: York returned with mugs of drink for Sacagawea and Charbonneau.

Charbonneau: Thank you.

York: You're welcome sir.

Charbonneau: The mountains are difficult to travel by foot. You will want to purchase the Shoshone's horses for safe travel over these mountains.

Clark: You believe the Shoshone will sell them to us?

Charbonneau: I believe if you have someone there who can speak their language, your chances are better.

Lewis: I would agree. We plan to leave in the spring. Is that suitable for you?

Charbonneau: Yes, it is.

Clark: The spring it is. Charbonneau and Sacagawea, welcome to the Corps of Discovery.

Scene Three
Setting: Fort Mandan.

Narrator 1: In March 1805, the soldiers prepared to leave Fort Mandan. Charbonneau approached Captains Lewis and Clark.

Charbonneau: If you want me to accompany you, I demand to be relieved of your required duties. There's no need for me to stand guard duty or report what personal items I plan to take.

Lewis: I appreciate your words Charbonneau, but we're a team. All members of the team work together, no one is above reporting for duty. We share tasks and responsibilities.

Charbonneau: You are a long way from home now, and things are quite different out here. I will give you the evening to think it over. You will meet my demands—or I quit.

Narrator 2: Charbonneau walked away from Lewis and Clark. Sacagawea was waiting for him, and holding their one-month-old son.

Sacagawea: Are we no longer going with them?

Charbonneau: Perhaps not. I refuse to do such menial work. They want an interpreter, that's what I am. And, that's all I am for them.

Sacagawea: Will they agree to your demands?

Charbonneau: I don't know.

Narrator 1: Later, Lewis and Clark approached Charbonneau and Sacagawea.

Lewis: We have discussed it, and you're free to quit if you like.

Clark: We will find another interpreter who will be a part of our team.

Charbonneau: You are allowing me to quit?

Lewis: Yes, we are.

Scene Four
Setting: Charbonneau's home.

Sacagawea: Are we traveling with them?

Charbonneau: I should just quit. But, I won't.

Sacagawea: So, should I prepare to leave?

Charbonneau: Yes. You should. We will go. The pay is too great, and I'll do their menial duties. We leave soon, and will bring the child.

Sacagawea: Yes, my husband.

Narrator 2: On April 7, 1805, the Corps of Discovery began their journey west. Lewis gathered everyone around before they left Fort Mandan.

Lewis: Today is a proud moment for the United States. Today, we venture forth into uncharted territory. We will learn of new lands, people, animals, plants, and more. Sounds we have never heard will be heard. Smells we have never breathed, we will inhale. And tastes we have never known, we will discover. So, let the adventure begin.

Clark: We will begin our journey heading up the Missouri River in our boats. Everyone climb in and let's go.

Sacagawea: Don't worry Pomp, we will have a fine journey. We'll see our people again, the Shoshone. I will teach you all I know of the land as we go.

Charbonneau: Sacagawea, we will ride together in this pirogue. It holds eight people.

Sacagawea: Let's begin our journey, Pomp.

Scene Five
Setting: At camp.

Narrator 1: Many days passed. The soldiers set up camp while Sacagawea tended to her son, Pomp. Pierre, one of the soldiers, came over to her.

Cruzette: That's a darling young boy you have.

Narrator 2: Sacagawea smiled, not understanding what the man was saying. He plucked a stringed instrument from his bag and played. Pomp laughed.

Sacagawea: Pomp, what an unusual sound this is.

Cruzette: It's a fiddle, Sacagawea.

Narrator 2: On the journey, Sacagawea understood only her husband's language and tried to learn the sounds spoken by the other men. She watched their food supplies dwindle day after day.

Narrator 1: Sacagawea knew the secrets of the land. She showed them where to find food. She, Pierre, and the other soldiers sat together and ate. Jerusalem artichokes grew nearby, and she left the group to gather them.

Pierre: Sacagawea, where are you going?

Frazier: She looks like she is picking something.

Sacagawea: Pomp, we will teach them to eat these plants. They should not go hungry.

Bratton: It's food. She's eating something, she must know it is a food.

Sacagawea: Pomp, we will bring them artichokes, as many as I can pick and hold.

Narrator 2: Sacagawea introduced Jerusalem artichokes to the soldiers. They looked like some sort of sunflower. The soldiers were grateful to have another kind of food to eat.

Narrator 1: Sacagwea's knowledge of the land and its available food was an invaluable asset to the success of the expedition.

Scene Six
Setting: On the river.

Narrator 1: Several days of traveling passed. On May 14, 1805, they were once again on the river. They traveled in several boats. In one of them, Charbonneau steered the craft along the river. Suddenly, a strong wind whipped across the waters.

Fields: The wind ripped the sail from my hands. The boat is rolling over. Quick, Charbonneau, turn the boat into the wind and lower the sails.

Charbonneau: I can't.

Narrator 1: Charbonneau froze with terror. He couldn't move.

Cruzette: You must! Quickly.

Narrator 2: The others watched from their boats in horror as the pirogue began to tip sideways. Private Frazier shouted from another boat.

Frazier: The medical supplies, food, and instruments are washing into the river. Someone get them.

Sacagawea: Pomp, stay close to me. We cannot let this precious cargo escape.

Narrator 1: Calmly, Sacagawea rescued the cargo from washing away. She swam into the water and curled her arms around boxes of the medical supplies, food, and instruments. She guided the boxes onto the shore.

Clark: Sacagawea saved the cargo. With a baby on her back, no less!

Narrator 2: Charbonneau was still frozen with fear and could not move. Lewis shouted across the water at him.

Lewis: Charbonneau. Grab that sail!

Charbonneau: I cannot move.

Fields: We need help!

Cruzette: I got the sail! Let's get this pirogue ashore. Charbonneau, help us get this boat ashore.

Charbonneau: I cannot move.

Fields: The danger is over, we're safe.

Sacagawea: Everything is safe. We didn't lose any supplies.

Narrator 2: Once ashore, Captain Lewis approached Charbonneau and Sacagawea.

Lewis: Thank you for saving our cargo, Sacagawea. That was very brave.

Charbonneau: She does not understand you.

Lewis: Then, tell her what I have said, Charbonneau. You're our interpreter. Interpret.

Sacagawea: Pomp, I believe this man has just expressed his thanks to me.

Scene Seven
Setting: Near the Rocky Mountains.

Narrator 1: The days continued to pass quickly and quietly. By midsummer, the river had become too shallow for them to stay afloat. They continued their journey on foot.

Narrator 2: As they approached the Rocky Mountains, Sacagawea began to recognize her homeland. She pointed to a formation jutting out from the valley floor.

Sacagawea: Charbonneau, tell them it is Beaver's Head.

Charbonneau: The Shoshone call this formation Beaver's Head. We are close to their home.

Lewis: We will meet the Shoshone soon. We must reach them before winter and use their horses to pass over these mountains. McNeal, Drewyer, and Shields come with me. We will look for the Shoshone and meet you back here.

Clark: Captain Lewis, are you sure?

Lewis: Captain Clark, look at our men. Many of them are sick and weak. They need rest. Our party of four can travel faster and make peace with the Shoshone.

Clark: I have heard they hide in trees, suspicious that all strangers are enemies.

Lewis: All the more reason for us to greet them, just four of us. Thirty-three strangers may be perceived as an enemy invasion.

Clark: And Sacagawea and Charbonneau?

Lewis: They will stay. She has traveled far with her young son. Let them rest and gather their strength.

Narrator 2: Lewis and his party set headed west to what we today call Lemhi Pass.

McNeal: I thought I just saw a Shoshone riding over there.

Drewyer: Where?

Shields: I see him. He's over there.

Lewis: Too far away. We could not hope to catch up to him that quickly. We are on foot, and he is on horseback.

Narrator 1: On August 12, 1805, Lewis unrolled the American flag.

Lewis: Perhaps now they will see we come in peace. Help me show the flag, so they can see.

McNeal: We can use this tree branch to tie it to.

Shields: A good make-do flagpole.

Drewyer: I think I see men approaching again.

Lewis: Where?

Shields: I see them, in the distance. I hope they know we are here in peace, because there are far more of them than there are of us.

Narrator 2: Sixty Shoshone on horses rode to where the American flag waved. The chief, Cameahwait, approached Lewis.

Lewis: Drewyer, I need you to tell him we are here in peace.

Drewyer: I will do my best.

Narrator 1: Drewyer used sign language to communicate with the chief. Cameahwait spoke to his people.

Cameahwait: We are safe. These people are not here to hurt us. They are here in peace.

Lewis: Drewyer, tell him to come with us to meet the others.

Narrator 2: Once again, Drewyer used his sign language skills to communicate with Chief Cameahwait.

Lewis: Well?

Drewyer: I think he has agreed.

Narrator 1: Chief Cameahwait spoke again to his people.

Cameahwait: They want us to meet the rest of their people. We will go, but stay alert. They have offered us peace, but let us not fall easily into a trap. We must be sure they are peaceful people and not let our guard down.

Scene Eight
Setting: Main camp.

Narrator 2: The Shoshone traveled with Lewis, McNeal, Shields, and Drewyer. Clark and the main party greeted them. A young Shoshone girl saw Sacagawea and ran to her.

Sacagawea: I thought you were captured as I was.

Shoshone girl: I was, but I escaped and ran home. You?

Sacagawea: I was sold to the Minataree.

Shoshone girl: We have missed you.

Sacagawea: And I have missed you too.

Shoshone: This is your son?

Sacagawea: This is young Pomp.

Narrator 2: Charbonneau came to Sacagawea.

Charbonneau: I cannot understand everything the chief is saying. They need you to interpret.

Sacagawea: Come with me.

Narrator 1: Sacagawea embraced her friend one more time before leaving her side. She sat with Clark and Lewis and looked into Cameahwait's familiar face.

Sacagawea: Cameahwait! My brother!

Cameahwait: Sacagawea, we thought you were lost forever.

Sacagawea: I've been traveling with these men. We have been traveling for many moons. You are chief?

Cameahwait: I am. I see you are a mother?

Sacagawea: I am, this is Pomp. Pomp, this is your uncle.

Cameahwait: It is good to see you again.

Lewis: Sacagawea?

Charbonneau: The chief is her brother. She has not seen him for many years.

Lewis: I see. Please ask Sacagawea to ask about the horses. We will leave them to their reunion. Captain Clark, shall we?

Clark: It seems we should.

Charbonneau: Sacagawea, talk to your brother about the horses.

Sacagawea: I will, Charbonneau.

Narrator 2: Charbonneau left Sacagawea and her brother alone.

Cameahwait: What is it he speaks of?

Sacagawea: Cameahwait, these men have come all this way to discover what lies west. They have never been over the mountains and need your horses to safely pass. These are good men, Cameahwait. They only want to learn about the land.

Cameahwait: I trust they are ready to propose a trade.

Sacagawea: I am sure they are. You have many horses. They would not need all of them. I also know they will try to cross the mountains with or without the horses. Without the horses, many of them will die.

Cameahwait: I trust your words. We will provide horses to complete their journey.

Sacagawea: Thank you, Cameahwait. My brother.

Cameahwait: Sacagawea, it is my belief these men would never have come this far without you. You know the secrets of the land, the people, and have led them to us.

Sacagawea: With or without me, these men would have traveled to discover the west.

Cameahwait: It is with you, Sacagawea, that they succeed.

Epilogue

Narrator 1: In November 1805, the Corps of Discovery saw the Pacific Ocean. They built Fort Clatsop and stayed there through the winter.

Narrator 2: In March 1806, they began their journey home.

Narrator 1: There are many historians today who disagree about the spelling of her name.

Narrator 2: The Lehmi Shoshone spell it Sacajawea, meaning boat launcher.

Narrator 1: The United States Mint printed the coin in her honor with the spelling Sacagawea, meaning bird woman in Hidatsa.

Narrator 1: They disagree on where she died. Some claim she died at the age of twenty-five in Fort Manuel, South Dakota.

Narrator 2: While others claim she died at the age of one hundred in Fort Washakie, Wyoming.

Narrator 1: While many disagreements and inconsistencies in stories written about her still persist, one fact remains true.

Narrator 2: She was a woman of strength, courage, and spirit who helped the Corps of Discovery fulfill their quest.

Narrator 1: In the journals of Lewis and Clark, her valuable contribution to the expedition is undeniable. No matter how we spell or say her name, Sacagawea was one of the reasons Lewis and Clark succeeded in the discovery of the west.

FOLLOW-UP ACTIVITIES

According to several resources, there was actually a fourth person in the interpretation chain of communication—Private Francois Labiche. Sacagawea spoke Hidatsa and Shoshone, Charbonneau spoke French and Hidatsa (not English). Since neither Lewis nor Clark spoke French, they called upon Private Francois Labiche to translate the French into English. The chain of communication was as follows: Sacagawea (Hidatsa), Charbonneau (Hidatsa to French), Labiche (French to English), and Lewis and Clark (understood English).

In the commonly known game "telephone," messages get changed when they are passed on in English. Imagine the challenge in communication when the message is passed through two translators and three languages.

A great activity to illustrate this chain of communication is to divide students into eight groups. Have each group take a scene and rewrite it, inserting Private Francois Labiche as the translator between Charbonneau and Lewis and/or Clark. What could get misunderstood? How do they resolve conflicts in the communication chain? Students may choose to perform their revised scenes to the rest of the class.

Another follow-up activity includes using improvisational theater games. Have students choose a member of the Corps of Discovery they want to be. If Sacagawea could speak English on the journey, what would she say? Use Improvisational Theater Situation exercises to explore what conversations may have occurred during 1804–1805. Some examples of situations may be:

• Pierre teaching Sacagawea how to play the fiddle

• Sacagawea talks to a soldier about her life as a Shoshone and why she misses it

• York and Sacagawea speak about being captives

Students may also prepare miniplays to perform for each other. Instead of these situations being improvised, students may plan what the situation will be, rehearse it, and perform the presentation for the rest of the class. For example, two to three students would choose characters to be from the Lewis and Clark expedition. They would decide on a problem that had to be solved. Together, they would write a script and rehearse it. Presentations may be three to ten minutes in length.

Another activity includes exploring the many controversies surrounding the actual historical events during the Lewis and Clark expedition. The play depicted one version of many for several historical facts. Students may choose one fact of the play and research other explanations of what happened. Students may research the following questions:

• Where did Sacagawea die?

• How did Lewis and Cameahwait initially make contact?

• Who supports spelling her name Sacajawea? How many different ways are there to spell her name?

• How did Sacagawea carry Pomp? On her back or in a wrap in front of her?

• How did Sacagawea become Toussaint's wife?

NOTE

1. It is unknown how Sacagawea carried Pomp. If she used the Shoshone method, she would have used a cradleboard. If she used the Hidatsa method, she would have used a blanket or shawl to carry him on her back.

REFERENCES

Adler, David A., and Dan Brown. *A Picture Book of Sacagawea*. New York: Holiday House, 2000.

Anderson, Irving W. *A Charbonneau Family Portrait*. Astoria, OR: Fort Clatsop Historical Association, 1988.

Bruchhag, Joseph. *Sacajawea*. San Diego, CA: Silver Whistle, 2000.

Clark, Ella E., and Margot Edmonds. *Sacagawea of the Lewis and Clark Expedition*. Berkeley: University of California Press, 1979.

DeVoto, Bernard. *The Journals of Lewis and Clark*. Boston, MA: Houghton Mifflin, 1953.

Herbert, Janis. *Lewis and Clark for Kids*. Chicago: Chicago Review Press, 2000.

Howard, Harold P. *Sacajawea*. Norman: University of Oklahoma Press, 1971.

Hunsaker, Joyce Badgley. *Sacagawea Speaks*. Guilford, CT: Twodot, 2001.

Lourie, Peter. *On the Trail of Sacagawea*. Honesdale, PA: Boyds Mill Press, 2001.

Pelz, Ruth. *Women of the Wild West*. Seattle, WA: Open Hand Publishing, 1995.

Rabbit Ears Productions. *Sacajawea*. Lancaster, PA: video, 1998.

Ronda, James P. *Lewis and Clark among the Indians*. Lincoln: University of Nebraska Press, 1984.

Sacagawea. New York, NY: Kids Discover Magazine, 2002.

Thomasma, Kenneth. *The Truth about Sacajawea*. Jackson, WY: Grandview Publishing Company, 1997.

Tinling, Marion. *Sacagawea's Son: The Life of Jean Baptiste Charbonneau*. Missoula, MT: Mountain Press Publishing Company, 2001.

Witteman, Barbara. *Sacagawea*. Mankata, MI: Bridgestone Books, 2002.

Chapter Three

Susan B. Anthony

(1820–1906)

Anthony's Fight for Women's Rights

BACKGROUND

The right to vote is quite possibly one of the important rights citizens of the United States possess. Less than one hundred years ago, women won the right to vote. Susan B. Anthony was an integral part of that victory. Over the past several decades, the number of people voting has steadily declined. In the 1996 presidential election, 54 percent of Americans who are voting age voted (Census Bureau of Statistics, 2000). This is the lowest percentage recorded in any presidential election since 1964.

Susan B. Anthony's story may inspire students to appreciate the importance of voting. Students may learn the impact their single vote has, thus instilling a sense of pride in voting. An important and valuable part of our freedom as Americans is to vote.

Susan Brownell Anthony was born February 15, 1820, to Lucy and Daniel Anthony. In a family of Quakers, she was the second of eight children. She grew up in Rochester, New York. She understood that society and the law did not treat men and women as equals and dedicated sixty years of her life to the cause of women's rights. In a time when women could not own property, keep their own wages, or vote, Anthony traveled the country lobbying support for women's rights. She remained a faithful activist until her death at the age of eighty-six.

This play depicts Susan's early childhood (1820s) through her death (1906).

PRESENTATION SUGGESTIONS

Susan B. Anthony should be center stage for this reading. The narrators may stand on either side of the stage and remain on stage the entire time. Characters who enter and exit the stage should stand next to Susan, whichever side you choose. If more than two characters are to come on stage, you may consider having them stand on either side of Susan. For scene two, you may want to have two chairs for Elizabeth Cady Stanton and Susan B. Anthony to sit.

For a backdrop, you may have students create a mural with the theme of women's rights. You can use mural paper and paste it against cardboard boxes. The mural could contain quotes from Susan B. Anthony, paintings of people from that time period, and/or voter registration cards.

PROPS (OPTIONAL)

1. Pen and paper, for when Susan is writing a letter
2. Handcuffs, for the Marshal to arrest Susan
3. Gavel, for Judge Hunt

LIST OF CHARACTERS

1. Narrator 1
2. Narrator 2
3. Susan B. Anthony
4. Elizabeth Cady Stanton, *women's activist*
5. Teacher
6. Daniel Anthony, *Susan's Father*
7. Man #1, *participant at Teachers' Convention*
8. Man #2, *participant at Teachers' Convention*
9. Man #3, *voter*
10. Man #4, *voter*
11. Man #5, *voter*
12. Woman #1, *participant in women's rights convention*
13. Woman #2, *participant in women's rights convention*
14. Sally Ann Hyatt, *worker in Daniel Anthony's mill*
15. Registrar
16. Marshal E. J. Keeny
17. Trolley Driver
18. Judge Hunt
19. Seldon, *Susan B. Anthony's lawyer*
20. Senator Argent, *Senator from California*
21. Politician #1

Optional:

Members of the jury, up to twelve

Additional voters in the registration office

‖ ANTHONY'S FIGHT FOR WOMEN'S RIGHTS ‖

Scene One
Setting: Susan's school.

Narrator 1: Susan B. Anthony was born in 1820 and learned early in her life that men and women did not share equal rights.

Narrator 2: She attended school with the other boys and girls. When she was eleven, she yearned to learn more. She approached her teacher with questions.

Susan: I noticed the boys were learning long division, could you please teach me?

Teacher: Susan, you know how to read, don't you?

Susan: Yes, I do.

Teacher: Long division is really quite complicated. It's something girls shouldn't be concerned with.

Susan: Yes, but I would like to learn long division. Could you please teach me?

Teacher: Now Susan, it's much too complicated for girls to learn. Why don't you practice sewing? Don't concern yourself with something you don't need to know.

Narrator 1: Frustrated with her teacher's unwillingness to teach her, Susan went home to tell her father.

Susan: My teacher refused to teach me long division just because I'm a girl.

Daniel: Unfortunately, many people think girls shouldn't have the same education as boys. That you should learn to cook, sew, and clean. Education is important, Susan.

Susan: I can learn just as much as any boy can.

Daniel: Yes, I know.

Susan: So, how can I learn if the teachers won't teach me? The boys get to learn everything, but they limit what the girls learn.

Daniel: I have an idea. We'll open a school where both boys and girls will learn all of the subjects together.

Susan: You can do that?

Daniel: I don't see why not. Girls and boys should receive an equal education.

Narrator 1: Daniel Anthony started the school, and taught some of the classes himself. He also ran a textile mill, where Susan often visited him.

Narrator 2: Susan loved to watch the workers in the mill. There was one worker she really admired, Sally Ann Hyatt.

Susan: Sally, how do you run this machine?

Narrator 1: Sally Ann was busy at her machine making cloth. The noise from the machine drowned out Susan's voice.

Narrator 2: Finally, it was time for a break and Sally stepped away from the machine.

Susan: Sally, how do you run this machine?

Sally: That would take too long to explain. But, if you want I can teach you how one day.

Susan: I would like that very much.

Narrator 1: Sally helped other workers when needed. All of the supervisors were men at the mill. Even though Sally Ann knew more about the machines and the work, she was never promoted to supervisor.

Narrator 2: Susan noticed this inequality and spoke with her father.

Susan: Why isn't Sally a supervisor?

Daniel: She can't be a supervisor Susan.

Susan: Why? She knows more than any of the other supervisors.

Daniel: True enough.

Susan: Then explain why she isn't a supervisor.

Daniel: She's a woman. Women cannot be supervisors. The workers would refuse to work for her.

Susan: That isn't fair.

Daniel: I realize that. But in today's world, that's the way it is.

Narrator 1: Susan still did not understand her father's explanation. She believed women and men should be treated as equals.

Narrator 2: Her deep respect for education motivated her to pursue a career in teaching. At the age of fifteen, she became a teacher.

Narrator 1: Men were paid three times as much than women to be teachers. But still, Susan believed in what she was doing. She attended a teachers' convention every year where only the men were allowed to speak. The women had to sit in the back of the room and were not allowed to participate, only listen.

Narrator 2: At one convention, men were complaining that they were not respected like lawyers, ministers, and doctors.

Man #1: It's ludicrous. The work we do teaching is valid and important. Why should a man who stands in a courtroom be respected any more than a man that stands in a classroom?

Man #2: I don't know. It seems when I tell people that I teach, I feel like they laugh behind my back.

Susan: Society says a woman has not brains enough to be a doctor, lawyer, or minister, but has ample ability to be a teacher. Don't you see, every man of you who chooses to teach admits that he has no more brains than a woman?

Narrator 2: From that time forward, Susan attended teachers conventions and campaigned for equal rights for women.

Scene Two
Setting: Elizabeth Cady Stanton's home.

Narrator 1: In 1851, Susan B. Anthony met Elizabeth Cady Stanton. Anthony believed in equal rights for humans, as did Stanton.

Narrator 2: Elizabeth invited Susan to visit her. They sat and talked about their experiences for hours.

Elizabeth: I remember the first time I realized women were not considered equal to men. My father was a lawyer. A woman came to him for help. She had lost her husband and was not entitled to any of the property he owned. She was left penniless.

Susan: Women do not have the right to own or inherit property. There was nothing she could do. I too have firsthand experience with the inequality between men and women. I have worked as a teacher for more than fifteen years and *know* that the male teachers are paid at least three times as much as female teachers.

Elizabeth: That's outrageous. That's why we held the first women's rights convention in Seneca Falls, New York. That was four years ago, and still women have no rights.

Susan: I do wish I could have attended the convention. Your Declaration of Women's Rights and Sentiments is infamous across the country.

Elizabeth: We haven't reached any of our goals yet. In the Declaration, we called for women to have the right to own property, speak freely, get a divorce, enter educational and professional fields just as men do, and, most important, vote.

Susan: How can they deny us the right to vote? We are not just house servants who cook, clean, and do the laundry. Women have able minds and deserve the right to vote just as any man does.

Elizabeth: I couldn't agree more. It's hard to spread the word out to citizens all over the country. I am married with children, and can't leave.

Susan: I have the freedom to travel since I have no children or husband. I could travel to towns rallying for the support of women's rights.

Elizabeth: We could do it together. I can write speeches and support you in your efforts.

Susan: There isn't anything I wouldn't do to ensure women have the same rights as men. Where do we start?

Narrator 1: The Women's Rights Movement took a thunderous step when Susan and Elizabeth befriended each other. They formed a lifelong friendship and team dedicated to women's rights.

Narrator 2: Elizabeth wrote the speeches and Susan delivered them. Susan traveled from town to town speaking of women's rights and rallying support.

Scene Three
Setting: The Women's Rights Convention in Albany, New York.

Narrator 1: In 1854, Susan attended the Women's Rights Convention in Albany, New York.

Narrator 2: A small crowd of women gathered around her to discuss women's rights.

Woman #1: I do extra sewing for other women in our town. My husband keeps all of the money I earn. He says it's the law.

Woman #2: My husband sold *my* jewelry to pay off *his* debt. Why should I lose *my* property because *he* owes money?

Susan: It is not right for men to own property when women cannot. It is not right for men to take their wives' wages, when it's you who earned that money. Elizabeth Cady Stanton and I are fighting for the Married Woman's Property Act, and you can help us. By signing our petition, you can tell legislature we deserve equal rights. We deserve to own property. We deserve to keep the money we earn. It is our right as citizens of the United States. I urge you today to sign and become a part of the Women's Rights Movement.

Narrator 2: Six thousand signatures were gathered for the petition. It demanded that legislature recognize the right for married women to own property. An additional four thousand signatures were collected for petitions requesting women be allowed to vote.

Narrator 1: The legislature rejected women's right to vote.

Narrator 2: Six years later in 1860, they did pass the Married Woman's Property Act. This act was a victory. It ensured that women could keep their wages, and own property without interference from their husbands. Elizabeth and Susan celebrated at Elizabeth's home over a pot of tea.

Elizabeth: Here's to an important victory, Susan.

Narrator 1: They held up their teacups in victory.

Susan: Although I am pleased with the passing of the Married Woman's Property Act, there's still a lot to be done for women's rights.

Elizabeth: I couldn't agree more. The passing of this act is one step towards a larger goal.

Susan: The world will never be right until women have the right to vote.

Scene Four
Setting: Voters Registrar's office.

Narrator 1: Susan B. Anthony wasn't done with her work. She marched into the voter registration office on November 1, 1872.

Narrator 2: After fighting for women's rights for the last twenty years, she was determined to cast a vote.

Susan: I would like to register to vote.

Narrator 1: The men in the office laughed at her.

Man #3: You can't vote. You're a woman.

Man #4: Everyone knows women belong in the home, cooking and cleaning. Voting is man's business.

Man #3: You should just go home.

Susan: I can prove I have the right to vote. According to the Fourteenth and Fifteenth Amendments of the U.S. Constitution, "All persons born or naturalized in the United States are citizens. The rights of citizens of the United States to vote shall not be denied or abridged on account of race, color or previous condition of servitude (slavery)."

Man #3: I don't know. I've never heard of a woman voting.

Susan: Do you deny the words of the Constitution? I was born in the United States, so am I not a citizen?

Man #4: I guess so.

Susan: Then, I would like to register to vote.

Narrator 2: Susan's name was entered on the voting list. On November 5, 1872, she went to the polls and voted.

Narrator: There were several men there placing their votes. They looked at her with curiosity.

Man #5: What are *you* doing here?

Susan: I have registered to vote. I am here to cast my vote for the president of the United States. I am a U.S. citizen and it is my right to vote.

Man #5: A woman voting? That's illegal.

Narrator 2: Anthony ignored the comments of the men and cast her vote for President Ulysses Grant. She bid good day to the men and left.

Narrator 1: Susan was thrilled that she was finally able to vote. She wrote her friend Elizabeth Cady Stanton of her success.

Susan: Well, I have gone and done it! I voted at seven o'clock this morning. What strides we have made!

Narrator 2: On November 28, 1872, Thanksgiving Day, there was a knock at the door.

Narrator 1: Susan opened the door and greeted Chief Marshal E. J. Keeny.

Marshal: Miss Anthony, I'm sorry for the inconvenience on such a holiday.

Susan: What can I do for you?

Marshal: Well, I'm here to deliver a warrant for your arrest.

Susan: For what crime?

Marshal: You voted. As you well know, it is against the law for women to vote.

Narrator 2: Susan took in a deep breath. Anger rose inside her. She thought to herself if she was to be arrested, she wanted everyone to know why. She thrusted her wrists toward the marshal.

Susan: All right then, put handcuffs on me.

Marshal: That will not be necessary Miss—

Susan: I insist. If voting is a criminal act, then treat me as a criminal. Handcuff me.

Narrator 1: The marshal reluctantly handcuffed Susan. At that time, there were no police cars so they took the trolley to the police station.

Trolley Driver: You must pay a fare, Miss.

Narrator 2: Susan was furious. She defiantly answered the driver.

Susan: I am traveling at the expense of the government. This gentleman is escorting me to jail. Ask him for my fare.

Narrator 1: The marshal paid her fare and took her down to the police station.

Narrator 2: A trial date was set for her crime.

Narrator 1: The trial began on June 17, 1873. She sat in the courtroom but was not allowed to testify in her own defense. The jury, judge, and lawyers were all men.

Narrator 2: The jury stared at Anthony as her lawyer, Judge Selden, spoke in her defense.

Selden: Miss Anthony committed no crime. As the Fourteenth and Fifteenth Amendments state, all citizens are entitled to vote. Miss Anthony was born in Adams, Massachusetts, and therefore is a U.S. citizen. This gives her the right to vote.

Narrator 1: Judge Hunt did not agree with the lawyer. He looked at the jury of twelve men and instructed them to find her guilty. The jury complied with Judge Hunt, and found Susan guilty.

Judge Hunt: Susan B. Anthony, you are charged guilty with the crime of voting illegally. You will pay a fine of $100 for this crime.

Susan: I will not pay a single cent of your unjustified fine.

Judge Hunt: Court is adjourned.

Narrator 2: All of the men glared at Susan as they left the courtroom.

Jury Member #1: Can you believe this woman thinks she can vote?

Jury Member #2: Women belong in the home. Cooking, cleaning, and caring for their husbands and children. They are not smart enough to vote. What's next, women as lawyers and doctors?

Narrator 1: The men laughed as they left the courtroom.

Narrator 2: Susan never did pay any of that fine.

Scene Five
Setting: Senator Aaron Sargent's office.

Narrator 1: Susan was determined to get women the right to vote. She met with politicians to try to get them to propose an amendment allowing women the right to vote.

Narrator 2: In 1878, she traveled 3,000 miles across the United States to meet with Senator Aaron Sargent in California.

Susan: Senator Sargent, thank you for seeing me.

Senator: Yes, Miss Anthony. I am aware of your speeches, and your fight. However, I'm not sure what I can do for you.

Susan: I just want you to propose the amendment allowing women the right to vote.

Senator: I'm not sure that would be wise. Not too long ago, we just passed the law allowing black men who are no longer slaves to vote.

Susan: I am well aware that black men acquired the right to vote. But, shouldn't the right to vote be available to all persons—regardless of their race *or* gender? Think about it, Senator, how many women live in California?

Senator: I don't know the statistics. Thousands I'm sure.

Susan: Thousands more votes for you, the senator who took a step forward for women's right to vote. Women do have able minds and opinions and should be granted the same privileges as men.

Senator: If I was to propose it, and I mean if, I cannot guarantee anything.

Susan: I understand. I just ask that you propose it.

Senator: Let me give it some thought, Miss Anthony. Thank you for coming in to see me.

Susan: Thank you, Senator.

Narrator 1: Senator Sargent did propose the amendment, but it was defeated.

Narrator 2: Susan asked politician after politician to support her cause. She continued to have the amendment proposed.

Politician #1: Miss Anthony, while I respect your efforts. Don't you think it's time you give up?

Susan: We have waited too long for the right to vote. Educated women have stood aside for decades while men continue to rob them of this right to vote.

Politician #1: I can't help you, Miss Anthony. Good luck and good-bye.

Narrator 1: Years passed, and Susan continued her crusade for women's rights.

Narrator 2: In 1890, the National American Woman Suffrage Association formed, and in 1892 Susan became the president. Women from all over the country banned together to fight for women's rights.

Narrator 1: In 1906, Susan attended her last National American Woman Suffrage Association convention. There, she celebrated her eighty-sixth birthday.

Susan: I have been fighting this fight for more than fifty years. We have come a very long way, but still women do not have the right to vote. It is time now to pass on this fight to a new generation. At this point, failure is impossible. Women *will* have the right to vote.

Epilogue

Narrator 1: Susan died March 13, 1906. At that time, only Wyoming, Utah, Colorado, and Idaho gave women the right to vote.

Narrator 2: In 1920, the Nineteenth Amendment gave women the right to vote in all states.

Narrator 1: Susan B. Anthony's fight for women's rights was at last won.

FOLLOW-UP ACTIVITIES

These follow-up activities are based on improvisational theater exercises discussed in Chapter Three. For further explanation of any of the games, please refer to that chapter.

For movement improvisational theater, students may create snapshots of events that happened. You may consider having all of the students write down one scene that could be a snapshot and put all of the snapshot suggestions into a hat. Have four students on stage, and draw one snapshot suggestion from the hat. Once you call it out, without talking, the students create that snapshot for the audience.

For example, one snapshot suggestion may be Judge Hunt finding Susan guilty. One student takes the place of the judge, one becomes Susan, another may be her lawyer, and the last student may represent a jury member. Snapshots are a great exercise for students to learn how to work together. Because students are not allowed to speak, it can be just as challenging as it is rewarding.

An interactive improvisational theater exercise is the Chair Game. Students may be a character from that time period to get someone out of the chair. Encourage students to portray real people from the time period that you have studied in class.

Susan B. Anthony and Elizabeth Stanton Cady started a newspaper, *The Revolution*, a women's suffrage paper. It was filled with stories of women and their accomplishments. Students can write stories for *The Revolution*. Choose a date for the newspaper, and have students create stories that may have happened in that time.

REFERENCES

Clinton, Susan. *The Story of Susan B. Anthony*. Chicago: Childrens Press, 1986.

Day, Jennifer C., and Avalaura L. Gaither. *Voting and Registration in the Election of November 1998*. U.S. Department of Commerce, Economics and Statistics Administration, August 2000.

Not for Ourselves Alone: The Story of Elizabeth Cady Stanton and Susan B. Anthony. Burns, Ken and Paul Barnes. 180 minutes. Burbank, CA, Warner Home Video: Public Broadcasting Services. Burbank, CA, 1999. Videocassette.

Parker, Barbara Keevil. *Susan B. Anthony Daring to Vote*. Brookfield, CT: Milbrook Press, 1998.

Chapter Four

Harriet Tubman

(1820–1913)

Harriet's Road to Freedom

BACKGROUND

Harriet Tubman was known as Minty as a child. She grew up to become one of the most renowned conductors on the Underground Railroad. Born a slave on a Maryland plantation, Harriet was frequently rented out to other plantation owners. She took the Underground Railroad to freedom and after that became conductor for the railroad herself. Fiercely dedicated to the freedom of slaves, she put her own life at risk many times to save others. She was known later in life as General Tubman and Moses because of her rescues of more than three hundred slaves.

This play depicts the early portion of her life and follows her road to freedom.

PRESENTATION SUGGESTIONS

Consider having Harriet put on a red bandanna at the point when she goes from being called Minty to Harriet. You may also want to have Francis and Harriet using real scrub brushes and buckets when scrubbing the floor. Jim and Harriet may use real hoes when hoeing the weeds in the field.

For a backdrop, cardboard can be used. Consider painting fields on the backdrop to give the feeling of being on a plantation. For staging, it may be more effective to have the narrators on opposite sides of the stage. Harriet may be center stage. As other characters move in and out of the play, Harriet may move stage left to make room for the additional characters.

PROPS (OPTIONAL)

1. Red bandanna
2. Pretend baby in a blanket, to be Miss Susan's baby
3. Two hoes
4. Bucket with scrub brushes
5. Muskrat trap
6. Washcloth
7. Bowl and spoon for cornmeal mush
8. Small piece of paper for the Quaker woman
9. Purse with coins in it for Mrs. Cook
10. Blanket

LIST OF CHARACTERS

1. Narrator 1
2. Narrator 2
3. Harriet Tubman, *a young girl who was a slave*
4. Mama Rit, *Harriet's mother*
5. Daddy Ben, *Harriet's father*
6. Edward Brodas, *Master on the plantation*
7. Mrs. James Cook, *a weaver*
8. Mr. James Cook, *a muskrat hunter*
9. Miss Susan, *Plantation owner*
10. Quaker woman, *part of the Underground Railroad*
11. Francis, *a house slave*
12. Jim, *a field slave*
13. Mama pig
14. Overseer, *watches over the slaves in the fields*

Optional:

Other slaves in the fields

piglets

‖ HARRIET'S ROAD TO FREEDOM ‖

Scene One
Setting: A plantation in Bucktown, Maryland.

Narrator 1: AraMinty Ross was born a slave on a plantation in Maryland in 1820. She was one of eleven children born to Ben and Rit Ross.

Narrator 2: Back then, young girls had a pet name.

Narrator 1: Hers was Minty.

Narrator 2: When girls became young women, they adopted their Christian name.

Narrator 1: Hers was Harriet.

Narrator 2: Minty slowly made her way back home from the fields. She had been carrying water to the slaves since sunrise. She talked to herself as she walked.

Harriet: Red leaves. Yellow leaves. It's harvest time. Harvest time again.

Narrator 1: Harriet approached her home, a small, windowless, one-room cabin. She heard Master Brodas shouting at her mother.

Master Brodas: Enough! She is my slave and I will rent her out if need be.

Mama Rit: Please Master Brodas, she's so young. You have already taken away so many of our children. Please don't take my Minty.

Narrator 2: Harriet froze in her steps. Master Brodas saw her and shouted.

Master Brodas: I'm sending you off to work for someone else. Come with me.

Mama Rit: No, please. She's just six years old.

Harriet: I don't want to go away!

Narrator 1: She ran past Master Brodas and into her mother's arms. Master Brodas was furious. He pulled Harriet from her mother.

Master Brodas: Enough of this nonsense. You are to come with me NOW.

Narrator 2: Master Brodas began to pull his whip out from his belt. Harriet reluctantly let go of her mother and followed Master Brodas. She sadly looked back at her mother.

Mama Rit: Be strong, my Minty, be strong.

Narrator 1: Harriet worried that she would never see her family again like her brothers and sisters. She bit her lower lip to keep from crying. Her mother went back into the small cabin as Master Brodas took Harriet away.

Narrator 2: The master brought Harriet to Mrs. Cook. She was a weaver. Although she made beautiful cloth, she was not a pleasant woman.

Master Brodas: Mrs. Cook, here is the girl I told you about. She will be able to help you with any of the tasks you need completed.

Narrator 1: Mrs. Cook glared at Harriet. She took money from her purse and handed it to Master Brodas.

Mrs. Cook: She'll do, I suppose. This is the payment we agreed upon.

Narrator 2: Master Brodas took the money and left.

Master Brodas: Good day, Mrs. Cook.

Narrator 2: Beautiful cloth lay all around the room. Mrs. Cook picked up a small piece of cornbread from the table and handed it to Harriet.

Mrs. Cook: Here is your supper. I don't want to hear anything from you. You will sleep on the floor in this room. I expect you to be ready to work in the morning.

Narrator 1: Mrs. Cook left Harriet in the cold dark room. She didn't even have a blanket or pillow.

Narrator 2: Outside the wind whistled through the trees. Harriet curled up on the cold hard floor and whispered to herself.

Harriet: I just want to be with my family again. Please.

Narrator 1: The next morning, Mrs. Cook woke Harriet with a sharp holler.

Mrs. Cook: Get up. You have work to do girl. Up now!

Harriet: Yes ma'am.

Narrator 2: Harriet slowly rose to her feet and rubbed her eyes. She felt her stomach growl with hunger.

Mrs. Cook: You will help me make cloth. Stand right over there. Here is your yarn. Take the yarn and wind it carefully. Don't pull too hard or it will break. I don't take to mistakes, so make sure you do it right the first time.

Harriet: Yes, ma'am.

Narrator 1: Mrs. Cook sat at her loom while Harriet held the yarn. Harriet worked day after day in that room. Winding yarn, she was careful not to break it for fear of being whipped. She watched the leaves on the trees from the window and quietly said to herself.

Harriet: Red leaves. Yellow leaves. I just want to be outside, be with my family again.

Narrator 2: Mrs. Cook didn't think Harriet worked fast enough.

Mrs. Cook: Stupid girl. You're no good to me in here. Let's see how you like working for the master.

Narrator 1: So, Harriet was put to work for Mr. James Cook. Her job was to check the muskrat traps to see if they were full. It was freezing and she didn't even have a coat or shoes to keep her warm.

Mr. Cook: You need to check the traps on the other side of the stream. Any full traps, bring them back to me.

Harriet: Yes sir.

Narrator 2: Harriet crossed the freezing water barefoot while Mr. Cook stood and watched. She found one full trap and brought it back to him.

Mr. Cook: I need someone who can move quickly. I can do the work faster myself.

Narrator 1: After many days of working in the freezing weather, Harriet became sick. She could hardly stand because she felt so weak.

Mr. Cook: You move slower and slower every day.

Narrator 2: Harriet coughed as a fever swelled inside her. She continued to work for Mr. Cook until finally her fever consumed her and she could no longer work. Mr. Cook decided he was done with her.

Mr. Cook: You're no good to me here. Back to Brodas you go.

Scene Two
Setting: In Rit and Ben Ross's cabin.

Narrator 1: Harriet was back home, in the small windowless cabin. She lay asleep on the hard floor as Mama Rit pressed a cloth onto Harriet's forehead. Daddy Ben shook out a blanket and placed it over Harriet to keep her warm.

Mama Rit: My Minty. So sick.

Daddy Ben: She looks like she is waking up. You're home now, Minty. With us again.

Harriet: Am I home?

Daddy Ben: Yes, you are. Just rest now.

Narrator 2: Harriet was relieved to be home again. Mama Rit cared for Harriet as much as she could.

Narrator 1: It took six weeks for Harriet to get well again. One evening she sat outside with her daddy.

Harriet: Daddy Ben, what do you reckon is beyond this farm and the fields?

Daddy Ben: I don't know, Minty. I suppose we'll never know.

Harriet: Don't you want to know?

Daddy Ben: You're awful young to ask such questions, Minty.

Harriet: The leaves are coming back onto the trees. It's almost seed time. I wonder if the trees past these farms look the same.

Daddy Ben: Maybe one day, if we're lucky, we'll know.

Harriet: You really think so?

Narrator 2: Daddy Ben stared into his daughter's innocent, pleading eyes.

Daddy Ben: You never know what might lie ahead of us, Minty. All we really know is we're here today. Tomorrow is an unknown.

Narrator 1: When Harriet turned seven years old, Master Brodas planned to rent out Harriet again. Mama Rit begged him to change his mind.

Master Brodas: Rit, I will not argue this with you. She has to go.

Mama Rit: Please, last time she got so sick. Let her stay with us, Master Brodas.

Harriet: Don't send me away again, Master Brodas. I want to stay here. Please!

Master Brodas: It's time. Now, give me that slave.

Narrator 2: Harriet held on to Daddy Ben with all her might. Daddy Ben leaned down toward her. Master Brodas tapped his whip.

Daddy Ben: Minty, we didn't even get to say good-bye to our other children. At least today, we can say good-bye.

Harriet: Daddy Ben, I don't want to go.

Daddy Ben: I know, but you have no choice.

Narrator 1: Daddy Ben let go of Harriet's hand. He turned his back and walked away. He sighed heavily as he and Rit left their little girl, again.

Scene Three
Setting: Miss Susan's plantation house. Harriet and Francis, another slave, are scrubbing the floor.

Narrator 1: Harriet's new master was Miss Susan. By day, Harriet was to clean the large plantation house. By night, she held Miss Susan's new baby.

Francis: We're lucky to work in this house. It's better than the fields.

Harriet: I don't think so. I'd rather be outside, working with Daddy Ben.

Francis: Doing man's work? I don't think so. I'd rather be right here, cleaning. It's not so bad really.

Harriet: Not so bad? We are not allowed to go outside when we want. I hardly get to sleep.

Francis: That would be hard. Up with that baby by night, cleaning by day. Maybe the fields would be kinder to you. But you're too little.

Harriet: I'm seven, that's not too little.

Francis: No? You look little to me.

Narrator 2: Miss Susan came into the room to check on the floor. Harriet and Francis stopped talking immediately. Miss Susan inspected the floor.

Miss Susan: This floor is still dirty. Do it again. If it's not clean by the next time I come in here, you'll both get whipped.

Francis: Yes, ma'am.

Harriet: Sorry, ma'am.

Narrator 1: Miss Susan stormed out of the room, leaving Francis and Harriet alone again. Harriet started to sniffle and quietly cry.

Francis: Now, don't go and do that. Miss Susan is just about as mean as they can get. We'll just scrub it all down again.

Harriet: I just want to go home, Francis. I just wish I could be home.

Francis: I know, Minty. We all wish we could be home. I was sold to Miss Susan three years ago. Left my mama and all my brothers and sisters. We all got sold to different masters. I consider myself lucky to be here in this house, where it doesn't get too cold or too hot. The work isn't as bad as others have it.

Harriet: I just want to be free.

Francis: Keep your voice down. You don't want anyone to hear you talk like that. You'd get the whipping of a lifetime!

Harriet: I don't care. I want to be free.

Narrator 2: The next day, Harriet was standing in the kitchen waiting for Miss Susan's orders for the day. A bowl of lump sugar sat on the table. Harriet had never had anything sweet before.

Miss Susan: You will dust the house today. I expect it to be spotless when we return from our walk.

Harriet: Yes, Missus.

Narrator 1: Miss Susan turned away from Harriet to put on her coat. Harriet reached for a lump of sugar. At that moment, Miss Susan turned back around.

Miss Susan: That's it! You are a useless, stupid slave girl.

Narrator 2: Harriet knew she was in for a whipping of a lifetime. She looked at the open door and ran.

Miss Susan: Stupid girl!

Narrator 1: Harriet knew the trouble she was in, but couldn't stand the thought of one more whipping from Miss Susan. She hid in a pigpen and stole scraps of food from the pigs. She whispered to herself.

Harriet: I don't know how much longer I can stay in this pigpen.

Mama Pig: (*snort*)

Narrator 2: For days, Harriet stayed there until she became so hungry that she returned back to the house. She meekly walked in the back door when Miss Susan saw her.

Miss Susan: You're not worth the money I'm paying for you! You're going back.

Narrator 1: Miss Susan returned Harriet to Master Brodas.

Master Brodas: Miss Susan. Why have you brought the slave girl here?

Miss Susan: This girl is not a house slave, she's completely useless. Put her to work in the fields.

Master Brodas: I'm so sorry Miss Susan. Maybe we can talk—

Miss Susan: I don't want to talk. There's nothing I want to hear from you or that I want to say. Good day to you.

Narrator 2: Miss Susan angrily left. Master Brodas stared at Harriet.

Master Brodas: I guess the only place left for you is in the fields.

Scene Four
Setting: In Mama Rit's and Daddy Ben's cabin.

Narrator 2: Back home again, Mama Rit was stirring a pot of cornmeal mush over a fire. Harriet was so relieved to be out of Miss Susan's house. The sound of that crying baby still rang in her ears.

Narrator 1: Mama Rit saw the scars from the beatings Miss Susan gave her.

Mama Rit: Minty, you have so many wounds.

Harriet: Miss Susan whipped me every time her baby cried. I couldn't stay awake all night to rock the baby, so the baby cried.

Daddy Ben: It's not your fault, Minty. It's not.

Harriet: I'm just happy to be home. I don't ever want to leave you both again.

Narrator 1: Rit brought Harriet a bowl of cornmeal mush. The first bite warmed her tired body.

Mama Rit: Pleasing those folks is next to impossible. They can do anything they want with you. Anything. Working in a master's house is better than the fields.

Harriet: I want to work in the fields. I want to be outside, breathe the air. It's closer to feeling free than being trapped in someone's house. Outside I can watch the sky, the trees, and even hear birds now and then. I want to work in the fields.

Daddy Ben: I think you're too little to work in the fields Minty.

Harriet: I'm not too little. I *can* work in the fields.

Narrator 2: Master Brodas took Miss Susan's advice and put Harriet to work in the fields. Harriet learned how to plow the ground, hoe the weeds, chop wood, and load the wagons. She tried to work as fast as the other workers, so the overseer wouldn't whip her.

Narrator 1: By the time she was eleven years old, she was working in the fields from sunup to sundown. One day, she was hoeing the weeds with the other slaves.

Jim: Harriet, you better move faster. The overseer is on his way.

Narrator 1: Harriet looked over her shoulder and saw the overseer marching toward her. She began to dig the hoe deep into the ground, pulling the weeds out of the earth.

Overseer: Keep it moving, girl. I will take the whip to you.

Harriet: Yes sir.

Narrator 2: The overseer stopped to watch Jim dig his hoe into the ground. He glared at Jim, so Jim began to work faster. At long last, the overseer left.

Jim: I can't stand it when he does that. Stares at us.

Harriet: He's not looking now. Stand up for a minute and look up.

Narrator 1: Jim kept working. Harriet stretched her back and looked into the sky.

Harriet: It's another beautiful day.

Jim: Harriet, what are you doin'?

Harriet: Breathing. The air outside is fresh and free.

Narrator 2: Jim watched Harriet. He looked into the same place in the sky she looked. He continued to work as he spoke.

Jim: You hear about that underground road?

Harriet: Stop lying Jim.

Jim: I'm not lying.

Harriet: A road that goes under the ground?

Jim: It's underground because it's a secret, and a way to freedom.

Harriet: Freedom?

Jim: Up North, black women and men are free. The road goes up North.

Harriet: How do you find this road?

Jim: Don't know.

Narrator 1: Harriet was thrilled to hear of an underground road. For years, she dreamed of freedom. She still worked in the fields, day after day, dreaming of the day she would find the underground road.

Narrator 2: When she was fourteen years old, an overseer threw a lead weight toward a runaway slave. He missed and hit Harriet by mistake. She was left with a large scar on her forehead and for the rest of her life had "sleeping spells." She continued to work in the fields, despite her spells.

Narrator 1: Her favorite days were the ones when she worked with Daddy Ben chopping the trees.

Harriet: I'm old enough now. It's time I wore a bandanna like the other women.

Daddy Ben: I agree. That's a nice bright red.

Harriet: Thanks. And I'm old enough to be called Harriet, Minty is a child's name.

Daddy Ben: Harriet, I have news. Master Brodas died. Our new master is John Stewart.

Harriet: I heard already Daddy Ben.

Narrator 2: Harriet stopped chopping the wood. She leaned on her ax and faced Daddy Ben.

Harriet: Don't worry about me, Daddy Ben. I can't be a slave my whole life. I plan to find that underground road and be free. Can you help me learn how to get along on my own?

Narrator 1: From that day forward, Daddy Ben taught Harriet all he knew about the woods, swamps, and rivers of Maryland. For fifteen more years, Harriet worked as a slave. She met and married John Tubman, a free black man. Even though her husband was free, Harriet was still a slave.

Narrator 2: One day when Harriet was headed home from the fields, a woman stopped her. She was dressed in a simple dark dress. Harriet recognized she was a Quaker. The woman softly called to Harriet.

Quaker: Harriet.

Harriet: How do you know my name?

Woman: From the scar on your forehead. I wanted to find you today because we Quakers have heard that Mr. Stewart is in need of money. He plans to sell you for a good price to a cotton plantation in the South.

Narrator 1: Harriet's eyes widened as she drew a deep breath.

Woman: We try to help slaves who want to be free. Harriet, take the underground road. It's not a real road, but it's the way to freedom in the North. In the North, slavery is illegal. So we call this road the Underground Railroad.

Harriet: How do I find this road?

Narrator 2: The woman handed Harriet a small piece of paper.

Woman: Give this paper to the first conductor on the Underground Railroad. The conductors are people who will help you move along the Underground Railroad. Follow the Choptank River forty miles to its beginning. Then follow the road to Camden, and look for the white house with green shutters. A conductor will help you there.

Harriet: Thank you, ma'am.

Narrator 1: The Quaker woman quietly slipped away. Harriet stared at the piece of paper, then quickly tucked it in her hand. She didn't want anyone to know her plans.

Harriet: I wonder if the leaves change color in the North. It won't matter to me if they do or don't. I'll be free. Soon, I'll be free.

Epilogue

Narrator 1: Harriet traveled roughly 157 miles on the Underground Railroad from Bucktown, Maryland, to Philadelphia, Pennsylvania.

Narrator 2: After she arrived in the North, she took a job in the kitchen of a hotel. But her dedication to free slaves never diminished. She became a conductor herself on the Underground Railroad.

Narrator 1: From 1850 to 1861, she made nineteen trips to the South. She led more than three hundred slaves to freedom even though there was a reward of $40,000 for Harriet's capture. That didn't stop her, and she continued her mission to free slaves.

Narrator 2: Slaves began to call her Moses because, like Moses, she led people out of captivity.

Narrator 1: Conductors on the Underground Railroad led more than 75,000 slaves to the North to freedom.

Narrator 2: Harriet Tubman devoted her life to the needs of others. In her lifetime, she was a nurse, spy, and a cook. In 1865, her dream of freedom came true. The Thirteenth Amendment was passed, outlawing slavery in all parts of the United States. Harriet died in Auburn, New York, in 1913 at the age of ninety-three.

FOLLOW-UP ACTIVITIES

These follow-up activities are based on the improvisational theatre exercises discussed in Chapter Two. For further explanation of any of the games, please refer to that chapter.

Use the Sculptures Game and have students create sculpture scenes from events that happened during this time period. Examples include scenes from the Civil War, slaves escaping through the forest, or the signing of the Thirteenth Amendment. You may want to discuss other events with students prior to doing the sculpture scenes.

Situation Improv offers the opportunity to further explore this time period. Ask students to write down three situations that could occur during Harriet's lifetime. Students then choose from a hat and improvise that situation.

Examples may include:

Working in the fields

Harriet reaching the North, what did she do first?

The signing of the Thirteenth Amendment

Two slaves preparing to escape

Harriet leading slaves to the Underground Railroad and one slave is afraid and won't continue

Have students create their own situations, and act them out. These activities are a great way for students to continue to use theatre to learn.

REFERENCES

Ferris, Jerri, and Karen Ritz. *Go Free or Die: A Story about Harriet Tubman.* Minneapolis, MI : Carolrhonda Books, 1988.

Petry, Ann. *Harriet Tubman: Conductor on the Underground Railroad.* New York: Pocket Books, 1955.

Schroeder, Alan, and Jerry Pickney. *My Minty.* New York: Puffin Books, 1996.

Taylor, M. W. *Harriet Tubman Antislavery Activist.* New York: Chelsea House Publishers, 1991.

Chapter Five

Elizabeth Blackwell
(1821–1910)

Elizabeth: The First Woman Doctor

BACKGROUND

Elizabeth was born in Bristol, England, and was the third of nine children. Her parents, Hannah and Samuel, believed girls and boys should receive an equal education. Therefore, the tutor for the children taught both the boys and girls the same subjects. This education for girls was unusual, in a time when young girls were only educated in how to cook, clean, and sew.

In 1832, the Blackwell family moved to the United States to pursue a better life. After her father, Samuel Blackwell, unexpectedly passed away, the family opened a boarding school. Elizabeth taught for several years, but was inspired to pursue a career in medicine. She paved the path for women to pursue careers in the medical field. She overcame numerous obstacles in her path to become the first woman doctor. She graduated from medical school at the top of her class in 1849 from Geneva College. In 1853, she opened a one-room clinic to serve poor women in New York City, and in 1857 it expanded to become the New York Infirmary for Women and Children.

Elizabeth wanted to offer opportunities to women to pursue the professions in the medical field. In 1868, the Women's Medical College of the New York Infirmary opened for women to study medicine.

This play depicts her life from the point she decided to pursue medicine to her graduation from Geneva Medical School.

PRESENTATION SUGGESTIONS

The narrators should remain on either side of the stage. Characters should enter and stand center stage. This play may be best presented first reading in a circle, with no movement at all. Students may then collectively decide on how to stand during the presentation.

PROPS (OPTIONAL)

1. Books for when Elizabeth studies
2. The letter from the Geneva College of Medicine

LIST OF CHARACTERS

If you have a larger class, have two students play Elizabeth, and divide the narrator parts among four students. If you have a smaller class, have students play multiple parts.

1. Narrator 1
2. Narrator 2
3. Elizabeth Blackwell
4. Mary Donaldson
5. Harriet Beecher Stowe
6. Dr. Jon Dickson
7. Dr. Elder
8. Mrs. Elder
9. Dr. Jackson
10. Dr. Darrach
11. Faculty #1
12. Faculty #2
13. Faculty #3
14. Student #1
15. Student #2
16. Student #3
17. Student #4
18. Registrar
19. Dr. Webster
20. Student #6
21. Student #7
22. Student #8
23. Physician #1
24. Physician #2
25. Physician #3
26. Anna Blackwell
27. Marian Blackwell
28. Mother
29. Dr. Benedict
30. Henry Blackwell
31. Dr. Hale

ELIZABETH: THE FIRST WOMAN DOCTOR

Scene One
Setting: Mary Donaldson's home.

Narrator 1: Elizabeth visited Mary Donaldson, a friend of her mother's who was dying from cancer.

Mary: Thank you, Elizabeth, for visiting me. Tell me, how is your family's boarding school?

Elizabeth: Just fine. It helps that I have so many brothers and sisters to run the school together. Every one of us does something for the school from teaching to cleaning the rooms.

Mary: You keep very busy with the school.

Elizabeth: We all keep busy. May I get you anything Ms. Donaldson?

Mary: No, thank you. What are your plans, Elizabeth?

Elizabeth: Plans? What do you mean?

Mary: Will you continue to teach at the school?

Elizabeth: Teaching is a noble profession, but I think I want something else. I'm not sure what that would be. Something that would engross my thoughts.

Mary: You should pursue medicine.

Elizabeth: Medicine? Surely, you must be joking. All doctors are men. Being a teacher is the only profession that women can pursue.

Mary: You can change that, Elizabeth.

Elizabeth: I'm not sure how. The sight of blood makes me nauseous.

Mary: You would get used to that. Elizabeth, you are an intelligent, determined, and compassionate woman.

Elizabeth: Thank you, Ms. Donaldson.

Mary: I am sure if a woman had treated my illness, I would not have suffered as greatly as I have. It is true there are no woman doctors, yet. Elizabeth, you would make a wonderful doctor.

Narrator 1: Elizabeth left Mary Donaldson's home to return to her own. Her sisters, Marian and Anna, were preparing dinner.

Elizabeth: I have wonderful news.

Marian: What?

Elizabeth: I am going to pursue a career in the medical field.

Anna: Become a nurse? Why?

Elizabeth: A nurse? No. A doctor.

Marian: A doctor? Only men are doctors, Elizabeth.

Elizabeth: I plan to change that. I am twenty-four years old, and I finally know what I want. I want to be a doctor.

Scene Two
Setting: Harriet Beecher Stowe's home.

Narrator 1: Elizabeth visited her neighbor, Harriet Beecher Stowe, to share the news of her plans.

Elizabeth: It was as if Ms. Donaldson had the answer I have been waiting for all my life. All of my brothers and sisters seem to know what they want.

Harriet: And being a doctor is your destiny?

Elizabeth: Yes.

Harriet: Don't be foolish, Elizabeth. That is far too hard of a road to travel.

Elizabeth: You're not alone in that thought. I have written several physicians in the field asking their advice. They all say it is impossible.

Harriet: A strong prejudice would exist toward you, Elizabeth. You must either crush it or be crushed by it.

Elizabeth: I know. It is the very idea that so many think it is impossible for a woman to become a doctor that inspires me to pursue it. Women need more opportunity to be a part of society.

Harriet: I cannot disagree with you that women need more opportunity. As long as you realize the enormous obstacles that lay in your path.

Elizabeth: I do. I have to raise $3,000 for medical school. I've accepted a music teaching position at a school in Asheville, North Carolina. The principal of the school used to be a doctor and I plan to study with him.

Harriet: Good luck, Elizabeth.

Scene Three
Setting: School in North Carolina.

Narrator 2: In June 1845, Elizabeth began teaching at a small school in North Carolina. Reverend John Dickson was the principal. He had agreed to help her.

Elizabeth: Thank you for having me at your school, Reverend Dickson. I appreciate your willingness to share your knowledge in the medical field with me.

John: You're most welcome, Elizabeth. I have a library of medical books you are welcome to study.

Elizabeth: A library full of medical books? That will be very helpful to me. Thank you so much for your generosity.

Narrator 1: Elizabeth taught music during the day and studied the medical books at night. After many months with the Dicksons, they began to call her Dr. Blackwell. Reverend Dickson became ill and overworked. He decided to close the school.

John: Dr. Elizabeth, I have referred you to teach music and study medicine with my brother at his school.

Elizabeth: Are you sure you don't want me to stay and help you?

John: No, you should continue your studies. I believe you will become a doctor one day, and I don't want you to stop pursuing it to help me. I have plenty of help here and will be fine.

Elizabeth: Thank you for your hospitality and having me at your school.

John: You're most welcome. My brother, Reverend Sam Dickson, is expecting you at his school in South Carolina. Good luck, Elizabeth.

Narrator 2: Elizabeth left Asheville, North Carolina, and journeyed to Charleston, South Carolina, where Dr. Samuel Dickson awaited her arrival.

Samuel: Elizabeth Blackwell, a pleasure to make your acquaintance. My brother thinks a great deal of you.

Elizabeth: Thank you, Reverend.

Narrator 2: Once again, Elizabeth taught by day and studied medicine by night. By May of 1847, she had saved enough money from teaching to devote her time to gaining entrance into medical school.

Scene Four
Setting: The Elder family home in Philadelphia, Pennsylvania.

Narrator 2: Elizabeth learned that Philadelphia was home to many of the well-known medical schools.

Narrator 1: She stayed with a Quaker couple, Dr. William Elder and his wife.

Dr. Elder: Elizabeth, you are best to gather advice from many professors and doctors in the field. They can be a great asset to you in applying to schools.

Elizabeth: I am creating a list of professors to visit. I am hopeful someone will offer meaningful advice in this process. At last I have enough money to attend medical school, but now I need to be accepted to one.

Mrs. Elder: Elizabeth, what you are doing will help all women after you pursue a career in medicine. No woman will have to travel such a difficult path again.

Dr. Elder: Keep persistent, Elizabeth. You will get into medical school.

Narrator 1: Elizabeth began visiting different professors in Philadelphia.

Narrator 2: She visited Dr. Jackson, one of the oldest professors in the city.

Dr. Jackson: Yes, ma'am, may I help you?

Elizabeth: Yes, I am interested in pursuing a degree in medicine. I have come for your advice on how to apply to medical school.

Dr. Jackson: You are joking, right?

Elizabeth: No, sir. I'm very serious.

Dr. Jackson: No woman has been admitted to medical school. I'm afraid I would not be very much help.

Narrator 2: Elizabeth would not give up. She continued to approach professors of medicine throughout the city. She went to Dr. Darrach, another professor of medicine.

Dr. Darrach: Yes, ma'am. May I help you?

Elizabeth: Yes, I am interested in acquiring information on how to get into medical school.

Narrator 2: Dr. Darrach stared at her in silence for a long time. Elizabeth waited for him to say something, anything.

Dr. Darrach: I'm afraid I have no opinion to offer you at this time.

Elizabeth: Can you refer me to other professors to speak with?

Dr. Darrach: No, I'm afraid that would be unadvisable.

Narrator 2: Elizabeth encountered the same discouraging answers professor after professor. She sat with the Elders and discussed her plight.

Elizabeth: None of these professors will give me any assistance. Still, there must be a way into medical school for me. Their reluctance makes me more determined than before to become a doctor.

Dr. Elder: You will find a way. I am sure of it.

Elizabeth: Do you know one doctor actually suggested I disguise myself as a man to get into school?

Dr. Elder: That does not surprise me in the least.

Elizabeth: I've already been studying on my own for several years now. I know I would make a good doctor.

Mrs. Elder: You will make a good doctor, Elizabeth. Keep pursuing this path. You are doing everything you can.

Elizabeth: Thank you so much, both of you, for letting me stay with you while I pursue admittance into medical school.

Dr. Elder: Have you applied to smaller colleges as well as the larger well known ones?

Elizabeth: No, I have not. Could you please suggest which ones?

Dr. Elder: Of course.

Narrator 2: Elizabeth applied to twenty-nine schools. One of those schools was Geneva Medical College in New York.

Scene Five
Setting: Geneva Medical College.

Narrator 2: The faculty at Geneva Medical College received Elizabeth's application for admittance. They discussed what to do with it.

Faculty #1: A woman wants to be a doctor. Shall we turn her down?

Faculty #2: No, let's have the students decide. I'm sure they will turn it down. And if the finger is pointed at us for not allowing a woman into our school, we can state it was the students' decision.

Faculty #3: Great idea, with the women's movement it would be wise to let the students decide they do not want a woman here than for us.

Narrator 1: The students received a copy of Elizabeth's application. They laughed at the very idea.

Student #1: A woman in medical school?

Student #2: The dean must be playing a joke on us.

Student #3: Must be.

Student #4: Sure, why not. Let's have a woman in our school. Let's create a document stating the door to education should be open to all.

Student #1: Let's write it up. Elizabeth Blackwell, welcome to Geneva Medical College!

Student #2: You really think the faculty will let her in?

Student #3: No way, I'm sure it is all one big joke. Let's play along.

Scene Six
Setting: Elders Home, then Geneva Medical College.

Narrator 1: On October 22, 1847, Elizabeth received a long white envelope. Mrs. Elder and Elizabeth sat by the fire as she began to open the letter.

Elizabeth: I am almost out of money; I hope this is an acceptance letter. Otherwise, I'm not sure what I will do.

Narrator 2: Elizabeth read the letter and drew in a large breath.

Mrs. Elder: Who is it from?

Elizabeth: Geneva Medical School. They have accepted my application to medical school!

Mrs. Elder: That's wonderful. Dr. Elder will be so excited to hear the news.

Narrator 2: Dr. Elder came into the room and joined them beside the fire. Mrs. Elder and Elizabeth were smiling and laughing.

Dr. Elder: What is happening here?

Elizabeth: I've been accepted to Geneva Medical School!

Dr. Elder: That's wonderful news!

Mrs. Elder: Congratulations Elizabeth. You are well on your way to becoming a doctor.

Elizabeth: I can't believe it. I will miss living in your wonderful home. You have both been so kind to me.

Mrs. Elder: One day you will become a famous doctor. We will be able to boast that you once lived in our home!

Narrator 2: Elizabeth laughed and looked at the letter again.

Elizabeth: Thank you both, so very much.

Dr. Elder: You are welcome. We are very proud of you, Elizabeth.

Narrator 1: On November 6, 1847, Elizabeth arrived at Geneva College as student number 130. People stared at her as she entered the building.

Elizabeth: Yes, I'm here to enroll in my classes.

Registrar: Your classes?

Elizabeth: Yes, I'm Elizabeth Blackwell. I was just accepted into your school. Here are my papers stating I was admitted.

Registrar: Yes, well. Everything here seems to be in order. Let me get your class schedule, and you will be on your way.

Elizabeth: Thank you.

Narrator 2: Elizabeth was so excited to have the first step in her dream come true. Medical school at last! She went to her classes, and particularly enjoyed her anatomy class.

Narrator 1: On one occasion, Dr. Webster asked Blackwell not to attend some of the demonstrations.

Dr. Webster: Elizabeth, I think you should stop attending some of my classes.

Elizabeth: Is that so? Why?

Dr. Webster: You're the only woman in the class. The demonstrations may be too much for a lady to handle.

Elizabeth: I don't think that is true.

Dr. Webster: We may be dissecting animals, or other demonstrations that might make you faint. If you were to faint, that would be a distraction to the other students. I only have your best interest in mind. I really believe it would be best for all students if you did not attend the demonstrations.

Elizabeth: Dr. Webster, I enjoy anatomy class. I am a student here as anyone else. Why don't you leave the decision up to the students in the class? I will wait in the other room while you propose the idea.

Dr. Webster: Very well.

Narrator 2: Dr. Webster approached the class, while Elizabeth listened in the other room.

Dr. Webster: Class, I would like your input on having Elizabeth absent from class.

Student #6: Why?

Dr. Webster: I believe she's a distraction to your studies. I believe she might not be able to handle some of the more detailed demonstrations.

Student #7: She's not a distraction.

Student #8: She is a student, like us.

Student #7: Elizabeth should be in class, with us.

Narrator 2: The students agreed that Elizabeth should remain in class. To Dr. Webster's dismay, Elizabeth returned to class. The subject was never brought up again.

Scene Seven
Setting: Blockley Almshouse.

Narrator 2: To gain some practical experience, Elizabeth worked at the Blockley Almshouse during her break between semesters. This house treated sick people who could not afford personalized medical care.

Narrator 1: The young physicians were discussing a patient when Elizabeth approached them.

Elizabeth: What can I do to help?

Physician #1: We don't need your help.

Physician #2: Shouldn't you be cleaning or cooking somewhere? Being a doctor is for men, not women.

Elizabeth: Not anymore, it's not. I am here to learn to complement my studies. May I remind you I am a medical student, and expect to be treated as such.

Physician #3: Fine. Why don't you check on my patient down the hall, last room.

Elizabeth: Thank you, I will. His chart is there?

Physician #3: Of course. Please give me your opinion on his current condition.

Narrator 2: Elizabeth walked down the hall to the last room as asked. When she entered the room, no one was there. There was no patient. She could hear the doctors laughing down the hall.

Elizabeth: I'll check on a different patient.

Narrator 1: Elizabeth went into the next room, only to find the patient's chart missing.

Elizabeth: I have no idea what this patient has or needs. Those foolish physicians hid the chart from me.

Narrator 2: Elizabeth continued working at the Almshouse, despite the unfriendly manner in which she was treated. Dr. Benedict didn't share the others' opinion and approached Elizabeth.

Dr. Benedict: You are a very hardworking young lady. I admire your determination.

Elizabeth: Thank you, Dr. Benedict.

Dr. Benedict: I realize some of the young physicians are giving you a hard time. Why don't you assist me in working with my next patient?

Elizabeth: Work with you? I would be honored.

Narrator 2: Elizabeth learned a great deal from Dr. Benedict and continued to assist him with his patients. The young doctors still gave Elizabeth a hard time, but Elizabeth was more determined than ever to learn and become the best doctor she could.

Scene Eight
Setting: House at the beach.

Narrator 2: Before beginning her second year of school, Elizabeth took a break with her sisters and mother. They stayed in a house on the beach together.

Elizabeth: I have just one year of school left, and then I will be a doctor.

Marian: How was working at the Blockley Almshouse?

Elizabeth: Terrible. I learned a lot, but most of the staff refused to pay any attention to me.

Anna: They just aren't ready to accept a woman being a doctor.

Mother: You'll help them overcome that notion.

Elizabeth: They hid charts from me, left the room when I entered, and showed no respect.

Marian: How very immature!

Anna: They just saw a woman, not a doctor.

Mother: How is school?

Elizabeth: It was hard at first, but the students and faculty seemed to accept me the longer I was there. I think some students forgot that I am a woman, and just saw another student.

Marian: That's progress.

Anna: You are helping women all over the world pursue becoming a doctor, if that is what they want.

Elizabeth: I still have a lot I want to do. I am thinking about becoming a surgeon.

Marian: Really? That's wonderful.

Mother: Your younger sister, Emily, is also thinking about medical school. You are quite a role model for her.

Elizabeth: Maybe we will work together, one day.

Scene Nine
Setting: Geneva Medical College.

Narrator 2: Elizabeth's last semester in medical school passed quickly. Before she knew it, graduation day arrived.

Narrator 1: Her brother, Henry, attended her graduation. He helped her get ready for the day.

Elizabeth: Will you please help me get ready? I'm so nervous.

Henry: What's to be nervous about? You are a doctor, Elizabeth. Today you become the first woman doctor.

Elizabeth: You are making me more nervous, Henry. Does this hat look okay to you?

Henry: It's a little crooked. It looks like something is on it.

Elizabeth: What? Where?

Henry: I'm just kidding! You look fine, Elizabeth. Just fine.

Elizabeth: Where are my gloves? I want to look perfect for today.

Narrator 2: Henry handed Elizabeth her gloves.

Elizabeth: Here they are. Now, we should go. We don't want to be late for my big day!

Narrator 1: Henry and Elizabeth entered the large church where the graduation is being held.

Narrator 2: Dr. Hale, the president of the University, addressed the students.

Dr. Hale: Graduating class of 1849, I welcome you into the medical profession as doctors. You have a great responsibility bestowed upon you. With the title of doctor comes a responsibility to aid the sick and continue to preserve life. In your pursuits,

I believe your studies at Geneva Medical College have prepared you for the life you have chosen—the life of a doctor.

Narrator 1: The students received their diplomas, and Elizabeth entered the stage to receive hers.

Dr. Hale: Elizabeth Blackwell, the top student in the class. Dr. Blackwell, good luck to you.

Elizabeth: Thank you. Truly, thank you. It shall be the efforts of my life to shed honor upon your diploma.

Narrator 2: Everyone at the graduation applauded for Elizabeth. For she was now, Dr. Elizabeth Blackwell—the first woman doctor.

Epilogue

Narrator 1: Elizabeth went on to pursue becoming a surgeon, but an eye injury left her blind in one eye. She went on to promote hygiene and preventative medicine, which became her focus for the remainder of her career.

Narrator 2: She practiced medicine in England for a short time and returned to the United States in 1851 to New York.

Narrator 1: In 1857, she opened the New York Infirmary for Indigent Women and Children to serve the poor. She also provided positions for female physicians and training.

Narrator 2: In 1868, she established a Women's Medical College, where she was one of the professors.

Narrator 1: She returned to England, and her sister Emily Blackwell continued to run the college. Elizabeth died May 31, 1910, at the age of eighty-nine.

FOLLOW-UP ACTIVITIES

Using improvisational theatre, students can further explore situations in the field of medicine. The theme can be specifically around Elizabeth Blackwell's life, or can expand to situations in the field of medicine. Using the game Freeze, students can start a scene that focuses on situations that might occur in the health field.

REFERENCES

Baker, Rachel. *The First Woman Doctor*. New York: Scholastic, 1961.

Blackwell, Elizabeth. *Pioneer Work in Opening the Medical Profession to Women*. New York: Source Book Press, 1895.

Curtis, Robert H. *Medicine Great Lives*. New York: Charles Scribner's Sons, 1993.

Henry, Joanne Landers, and Robert Doremus. *Elizabeth Blackwell Girl Doctor*. New York: Aladdin Paperbacks, 1961.

Kerr, Laura. *Doctor Elizabeth*. New York: Thomas Nelson and Sons, 1946.

Sabin, Francene, and Ann Toulmin-Rothe. *Elizabeth Blackwell: The First Woman Doctor*. Mahwah, NJ: Troll Associates, 1982.

Schliechert, Elizabeth, and Antonio Castro. *The Life of Elizabeth Blackwell*. Breckenridge, CO: Twenty First Century Books, 1992.

Stille, Darlene R. *Extraordinary Women of Medicine*. New York: Children's Press, 1997.

Chapter Six

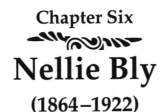

Nellie Bly

(1864–1922)

The Tale of Nellie Bly

BACKGROUND

In the late 1800s, men dominated the world of journalism. Elizabeth Cochran, later known as Nellie Bly, stormed into the reporting arena and changed its course forever. Born in a time where career opportunities were few and far between for women, Nellie Bly made history with her investigative reporting tactics.

She posed as a mentally ill woman to experience and write about a women's mental hospital. She went undercover working in factories and exposed the harsh working conditions laborers endured. As a reporter for the *New York World* newspaper, she sought out opportunities to experience and write about adventure. She decided to break the fictional record of eighty days around the world, as captured in Jules Verne's book *Around the World in 80 Days.* She completed her journey around the world in seventy-two days, writing stories along the way. Her determination and savvy stunt reporting broke ground for women to gain acceptance in the field of journalism.

This play depicts Nellie's life from when she began writing for the *Dispatch,* when she was twenty-one years old (1885) to her seventy-two days around the world adventure (1890).

PRESENTATION SUGGESTIONS

Nellie should be center stage for this reading. The narrators may stand on either side of the stage and remain on stage the entire time. Characters who enter and exit the stage should stand next to Nellie, whichever side you choose. If more than two characters are to come on stage, you may consider having them stand on either side of Nellie.

For a backdrop, you may have students create a mural with the route she took for her trip around the world in seventy-two days.

LIST OF CHARACTERS

1. Narrator 1
2. Narrator 2
3. Elizabeth Cochrane, *known as Nellie Bly*
4. Jane, *a friend of Elizabeth Cochrane's*
5. Assistant Editor at the *Dispatch*
6. Erasmus Wilson, *reporter* at the *Dispatch*

7. George Malden, *editor at the* Dispatch
8. Woman #1, *factory worker*
9. Woman #2, *factory worker*
10. Woman #3, *factory worker*
11. Woman #4, *factory worker*
12. Woman #5, *factory worker*
13. Woman #6, *factory worker*
14. Woman #7, *factory worker*
15. Factory Boss
16. Child, *factory worker*
17. Joaquin Miller, *American poet*
18. Ticket Station Manager in Mexico
19. Office Boy at *New York World* magazine
20. Reporter at *New York World* magazine
21. Joseph Pulitzer, *editor of* New York World *magazine*
22. John Cockerill, *managing editor of* New York World *magazine*
23. Doctor, *at Blackwell's Island*
24. Nurse, *at Blackwell's Island*
25. Lawyer from *New York World* magazine
26. Blackwell Woman #1, *at Blackwell's Island*
27. Blackwell Woman #2, *at Blackwell's Island*
28. Jules Verne, *author of* Around the World in 80 Days
29. Hotel Manager, *in Hong Kong*

PROPS (OPTIONAL)

Newspaper for scene one

||| THE TALE OF NELLIE BLY |||

Scene One
Setting: In a park in Pittsburgh, Pennsylvania.

Narrator 1: In 1884, there were not many jobs for women. Choices were limited, and Elizabeth Cochrane, later known as Nellie Bly, was one of the women in the 1880s in a job she did not enjoy.

Narrator 2: When she wasn't ironing or steaming clothes at her job, she visited with her friend Jane. They enjoyed reading the newspaper and discussing the articles.

Nellie: I would really like to write for one of these newspapers one day.

Jane: How? All of the writers are men. Women aren't allowed to do anything, really.

Nellie: Look at this article.

Jane: Which one?

Nellie: This one here, written by an Erasmus Wilson. He goes on and on about women and how we should not seek out any careers that are *male* professions.

Jane: Male professions? Which would be?

Nellie: Anything interesting of course. Apparently, Mr. Wilson thinks women should only cook, clean, and raise obedient children. Look at the title of the article "What Are Girls Good For?"

Jane: Is that so?

Nellie: I think I'll write this so called reporter a letter and tell him what I think about his beliefs.

Jane: There you go!

Narrator 2: Nellie wrote that letter and the editor of the *Dispatch*, George Madden, received it.

Narrator 1: The letter explained how it is impossible for a woman living in 1885 to find work and was signed Lonely Orphan Girl. George discussed it with his assistant editor.

George: Look at the spirit in this letter.

Assistant Editor: What?

George: I want this girl to work here. Her punctuation is terrible. Her grammar is a disgrace. But she can really capture the spirit!

Assistant Editor: It's signed Lonely Orphan Girl. How will you find her?

George: We'll run an ad in our next paper. We'll invite the Lonely Orphan Girl to come to the paper and identify herself.

Assistant: Whatever you say, boss.

Scene Two
Setting: The **Dispatch** *offices.*

Narrator 1: Nellie arrived at the *Dispatch* office, not knowing what to expect.

Narrator 2: Erasmus Wilson and George Madden greeted her.

Erasmus: I guess my column got a bit under your skin.

Nellie: I think that's evident by my reply, don't you think, Mr. Wilson?

George: We were very impressed with the spirit of your writing. In fact, we would like to offer you a job.

Nellie: A job? Doing what?

George: A reporter. We'd like you to be a writer for the *Dispatch*.

Nellie: When do I start?

Narrator 1: Elizabeth was thrilled to begin her career as a journalist.

Narrator 2: She decided the name Elizabeth Cochrane didn't quite fit her new career. She chose the pen name "Nellie Bly." It was the title of a popular song by Stephen Foster.

Narrator 1: She took the reporting world by storm with her strong opinions and fearless language. In one story, she wanted to investigate working conditions for women in factories. She discussed this idea with George.

Nellie: Pittsburgh factories employ hundreds of women. I would like to investigate their working conditions.

George: Sounds like a good story to me.

Scene Three
Setting: Factory in Pittsburgh.

Narrator 1: Nellie visited factories that produced bread, shoes, cigars, and other products.

Narrator 2: On one visit to a clothing factory, she met and talked with several women.

Woman #1: We work longer hours than the men here, and for less pay.

Woman #2: But it's worth it. One day women will receive equal rights in the workplace.

Nellie: So, is that why you do it?

Woman #3: For me, I don't want to rely on a man. I'm not willing to marry just anyone. It's hard to find work as a woman, but it would be harder to be married to someone I didn't even like.

Woman #4: That's the truth. Women have no choices for work. So, we are left with these arduous jobs that barely cover our living expenses.

Narrator 2: Nellie also visited with women that worked at a tin factory.

Woman #5: Do you know if we're one minute late, they fine us?

Woman #6: Not just for that, they whittle away at our paychecks with absurd penalties.

Nellie: Like what?

Woman #6: If we speak to someone else or don't produce enough products that day, they take it out of our paycheck. We have no protection against these penalties.

Narrator 1: Nellie found some factories wouldn't allow reporters in. She decided to apply for a job at one of these factories to learn more from direct experience.

Factory Boss: Why do you want to work here?

Nellie: I need a job.

Factory Boss: Don't you have a husband?

Nellie: No, I don't. I need to make money on my own. I will work very hard for you.

Factory Boss: Okay, we'll give you a try. You can start today.

Narrator 2: Nellie was sent into a crowded hot room with hundreds of other women all cutting copper cable and winding it around large spools. Nellie talked with another worker.

Nellie: What do we do?

Woman #7: Just wind the copper wire around the spool and don't talk. We get into trouble for talking.

Narrator 1: Nellie worked for many hours in that room. She spoke to small child who was working as well.

Nellie: Do you work here every day?

Child: Yes, my family needs the money.

Factory Boss: There's to be no talking while working. It slows everyone down.

Narrator 1: Nellie didn't understand why children would be working in a factory. She questioned the factory boss.

Nellie: Why do you have children working here?

Factory Boss: If you want to work here another day, you will not say another word.

Nellie: Is that a rat I see crawling over there?

Factory Boss: You're fired. Don't come back.

Narrator 2: Nellie went home and finished an article "Our Workshop Girls," exposing the real working conditions in the factories of Pittsburgh and the need to improve working conditions for women and to enact stricter labor laws for children.

Narrator 1: At the age of twenty-one, she became known as one of the most important reporters in the city.

Scene Four
Setting: The **Dispatch.**

Narrator 1: Nellie's stories were creating havoc for some companies that advertised with the *Dispatch.* They threatened to stop advertising in the newspaper unless Nellie Bly's stories stopped.

Narrator 2: George felt he had no choice except to have Nellie write about "safe" stories.

George: Nellie, I would like you to start writing some stories about the fashion industry and performing arts. There's a flower show this weekend I want you attend.

Nellie: A flower show? That's doesn't seem particularly interesting to me.

George: It is to our readers. Cover the story.

Narrator 2: With no further explanation than that, she was expected to write about society, fashion shows, and other routine events.

Narrator 2: Nellie did not enjoy these new assignments. She yearned for more interesting stories. She became fascinated with the idea of becoming a foreign correspondent in Mexico. She pitched her story idea to George.

George: You want to travel to Mexico?

Nellie: Yes! I can bring Mexico to life in Pittsburgh. The politics. The people. The culture. The articles would undoubtedly sell more newspapers. I'm sure of it.

George: Then, I can't argue with you. Bon voyage!

Nellie: I'll pack my bags and be on the train by morning.

Scene Five
Setting: 1886, Mexico.

Narrator 1: Elizabeth spent six months in Mexico and traveled all over the country. She wrote about the Mexican culture and sent the letters to the *Dispatch* to be published.

Narrator 2: She met the American poet, Joaquin Miller, in her travels.

Joaquin: You've come to write about Mexico, have you?

Nellie: Yes. It's fascinating to me. I've been to carnivals, museums, and out to the countryside. It's quite beautiful.

Joaquin: What else have you discovered?

Nellie: I discovered some corrupt practices within the government.

Joaquin: Be careful what you investigate. You might want to stick to the food, carnivals, and museums.

Nellie: But there's a story here. Some reporters have even been thrown into jail so they can't write about what's happening.

Joaquin: And what is it that is happening?

Nellie: I don't know for sure, I just know it's very suspicious.

Narrator 2: Nellie was disturbed to learn about these reporters being thrown in jail and she suspected corruption in the Mexican government. She wrote about her opinions in the articles she sent to the *Dispatch*. The articles raised so much interest, other American newspapers ran them as well. Some of the Mexican government officials saw them and were very angry.

Narrator 1: Nellie realized she could be in trouble. She packed her bags and entered the train station.

Nellie: One ticket for Pittsburgh, Pennsylvania, please.

Ticket Station Manager: Si, señorita. Buen Viaje.

Narrator 2: Nellie breathed a sigh of relief as the train crossed the border back into the United States.

Scene Six
Setting: New York.

Narrator 2: Nellie decided Pittsburgh was too small for her and that it was time to become a reporter for a newspaper in New York.

Narrator 1: The paper she was most interested in was the *New York World*. She had been trying to get an appointment with the editor Joseph Pulitzer for many months, to no avail. Finally, she decided to stay in the newspaper offices until he agreed to meet with her.

Narrator 2: She warned the office boy of her intentions.

Nellie: I am not leaving this building until I speak with Mr. Pulitzer.

Office Boy: Madam, I do not know when that will be. You may want to come another day, or write him a letter requesting an appointment.

Nellie: I've already done that, he did not respond. I'm not leaving until I see him today.

Reporter #1: Maybe you should do as he asks, come back another time, Miss.

Nellie: Thank you so much for your suggestion, but I am staying.

Narrator 2: She waited for hours and then decided it was time to simply walk into Mr. Pulitzer's office where he was meeting with his managing editor. The office boy followed her.

Nellie: Mr. Pulitzer?

Office Boy: I'm sorry, sir. I tried to stop her.

Joseph: Who are you?

Nellie: My name is Elizabeth Cochrane, but people know me as Nellie Bly. I am interested in writing for the *New York World*.

Joseph: Is that so?

John: I'm John Cockerill, the managing editor here. We don't normally hire women.

Nellie: No? Well, I've been writing for the *Dispatch* in Pittsburgh. I have experience.

Joseph: Go on, young lady.

Nellie: I wrote about the real working conditions for women in factories. I went to Mexico and did a series of articles about the people and the culture there. I even exposed scandals in their government. I have an idea for the *New York World*. I'm sure your readers would like to know what really happens in Blackwell's Island.

Joseph: The mental hospital for women?

Nellie: That's the one.

John: Many reporters have already done that story. They all found it to be a good place for women who are mentally sick to heal.

Nellie: Those reporters were all men. There's a lot they could never see. As a woman, I can pretend to be insane and see how they're really treated. The real story behind Blackwell's Island. I'll spend one week there, after which time I would ask you to get me out. The story would be yours, exclusively.

Joseph: That sounds like quite an angle, Miss Cochrane. It's a deal.

Narrator 2: With one handshake, Nellie and Joseph agreed on the plan.

Scene Seven
Setting: Blackwell's Island.

Narrator 1: Nellie had successfully gotten herself admitted to Blackwell's Island under the name Nellie Brown.

Narrator 2: She sat at a long table with other women for dinner.

Nellie: Is it always this crowded in here?

Blackwell Woman #1: They pack us in here like rats.

Blackwell Woman #2: They treat us like rats too.

Nurse: Dinner's ready.

Narrator 2: Nellie watched the women grab moldy bread from the plates. A staff member served a small amount of meat onto each person's plate.

Nellie: What's this?

Blackwell Woman #2: Dinner. Every night it's the same.

Nellie: What is the staff eating?

Blackwell Woman #1: Them? Oh, they eat quite well, they do. Large steaks. Fat potatoes.

Narrator 2: Nellie peered down at the end of the table. She saw the nurses and doctors eating steaks and potatoes.

Nellie: This is ridiculous.

Blackwell Woman #1: You think this is bad. Wait until after dinner.

Nellie: What happens then?

Blackwell Woman #2: They dump buckets of cold water on us and call it a bath.

Blackwell Woman #1: Not even time to dry off, just put on a thin nightgown and off to bed.

Narrator 2: After seven days in Blackwell Island, Nellie became a bit frantic since no one from the *New York World* came to release her. She begged her doctor to release her.

Nellie: You have to believe me. I'm here by mistake. I need to leave—now!

Doctor: Everyone says that, Ms. Brown. You are sick, very sick. We'll know when you're ready to leave. Believe me, you need to be here.

Nellie: No, I don't!

Narrator 2: After nine more days, she worried no one would ever come and get her out. She begged the nurse for help.

Nellie: Please, I'm not supposed to be here.

Nurse: You know, everyone says that.

Blackwell Woman #2: I'm not supposed to be here either. I've been saying that for five years.

Nurse: You've been saying that for one year, let's not exaggerate.

Narrator 1: After ten days, a lawyer from the *New York World* magazine arrived.

Lawyer: Ready to come home?

Nellie: Yes, I expected you at the end of a week, not after ten days.

Lawyer: Well, I'm here now. Do you want to leave?

Nellie: Absolutely. Let's go!

Narrator 2: After writing her story, Nellie returned to the office of the *New York World*.

Joseph: Your story about Blackwell Island was a hit. It seems that as a result of your stories, Blackwell Island and other mental hospitals are being investigated for their inhumane conditions.

Nellie: I'm glad something came out of that. The conditions in that rattrap were abominable.

Joseph: I'd like to hire you full time, as a reporter for the *New York World.*

Nellie: When do I start?

Joseph: Right now, Miss Bly.

Scene Eight
Setting: **New York World** *magazine offices.*

Narrator 1: Nellie continued to write under the name Nellie Bly for the *New York World*. After two years, she decided to go around the world. She wanted to try and beat the record of Phileas Fogg.

Narrator 2: Phileas Fogg is a fictional character from the book *Around the World in 80 Days,* written by French novelist Jules Verne.

Joseph: You want to travel around the world?

Nellie: In eighty days or less. People will love following me to places all over the world. I'm sure I can beat Phileas Fogg.

John: Phileas Fogg isn't even a real person, he's from a book!

Nellie: That's part of the fun!

Joseph: Okay, let's run with it. Pack your bags, Nellie Bly. You're traveling the world.

Narrator 2: On November 14, 1889, Nellie boarded the *August Victoria* to England. She traveled on trains and ships. Her trip took place before airplanes were an established mode of transportation.

Narrator 1: After she arrived in England, she learned Jules Verne wanted to meet her. She took a detour to France to meet him.

Jules: So nice to meet you, Nellie Bly.

Nellie: You as well.

Jules: So, you plan to beat my Phileas Fogg's record? Tell me where you plan to go.

Nellie: From here, I will go south to Italy, through Africa, cross the Indian Ocean. Then, I will travel to China and then across the Pacific Ocean.

Jules: You will come into the port of San Francisco?

Nellie: Exactly. I will then travel by train across the United States until I reach New York again, arriving in eighty days or less.

Jules: Well, I wish you luck! Thank you for taking time out of your busy route to meet me.

Nellie: I wouldn't miss the opportunity to meet you, Mr. Verne.

Narrator 2: Nellie continued her travels, watching the time closely.

Narrator 1: She arrived in Hong Kong and checked into her hotel.

Hotel Manager: You're Nellie Bly?

Nellie: Yes, I am.

Hotel Manager: We know about your race around the world. Elizabeth Bisland was here days ago.

Nellie: She's the editor of *Cosmopolitan Magazine*.

Hotel Manager: She's traveling around the world too.

Nellie: What?

Hotel Manager: She started by going across the Pacific Ocean. She might beat you.

Nellie: Oh, I don't think so.

Narrator 2: Nellie was as determined as ever to get back to the states. She didn't want another reporter to beat her. She boarded the ship *Oceanic* in Japan and was greeted by the captain.

Captain: Nellie Bly, I presume?

Nellie: Yes, I am. No delays in getting started I hope?

Captain: No, not at all. We've been reading about your travels through Europe and Africa. Now you're here. We've even made a sign for you.

Nellie: Where?

Captain: In the engine room, over here.

Nellie: I like what you've written, For Nellie Bly, Win or Die.

Captain: We'll get you across the Pacific Ocean and in San Francisco before you know it!

Nellie: Let's go!

Narrator 2: The captain kept his promise. They arrived in San Francisco, and from there Nellie traveled the United States by train. She arrived in Jersey City on January 26, 1890. George greeted her at the train station.

George: Welcome home, Nellie! You beat Phileas Fogg's time!

Nellie: Was there ever any doubt?

George: Your time was 72 days, 6 hours, and 11 minutes. Well done! That editor from the *Cosmopolitan Magazine* still hasn't reached her end destination.

Nellie: Thanks, George. What's my next writing assignment?

Epilogue

Narrator 1: Nellie wrote a book about her travels, *Around the World in 72 Days.*

Narrator 2: In 1895, she married Robert L. Seaman.

Narrator 1: When he passed away, she ran his business, the Iron Clad Manufacturing.

Narrator 2: After several years, the company went bankrupt, and she returned to her first love—reporting.

Narrator 1: In 1914, she became a news correspondent during World War I.

Narrator 2: In 1919, she returned to New York and wrote for the *Evening Journal* on the needs of homeless children.

Narrator 1: She continued to write until her death in 1922.

FOLLOW-UP ACTIVITIES

Students may engage in a research project focused around Nellie Bly's trip in seventy-two days. The major stops along her record-breaking journey include:

1. Ameins, France
2. London, England
3. Brindisi, Italy
4. Port Said, Egypt
5. Aden, Yemen
6. Colombo, Ceylon (now known as Sri Lanka)
7. Singapore
8. Hong Kong, China
9. Yokohama, Japan
10. San Francisco, United States
11. Jersey City, New York, United States

Once each group has been assigned a location, they should answer the following research questions:

- Where is this city/country?
- What types of food do the people eat?
- What language do they speak?
- What kind of work is available?
- What's the dominant religion in this area?
- What kind of government do they have?
- What recreational activities exist?
- What kinds of sports do people play?

After the research is completed, students may share the information in a variety of ways. They may (1) create a short play about this location, (2) construct a scene of what Nellie Bly might have experienced in this location, (3) write a report, (4) present an oral report about the location, and/or (5) make an art project that represents this location.

REFERENCES

Ehrlich, Elizabeth. *American Women of Achievement: Nellie Bly.* New York: Chelsea House Publishers, 1989.

Emerson, Kathy Lynn. *Making Headlines: A Biography of Nellie Bly.* Minneapolis, MN: Dillon Press, 1989.

Kendall, Martha E. *Nellie Bly: Reporter for the World.* Brookfield, CT: Millbrook Press, 1992.

Quakenbush, Robert. *Stop the Presses, Nellie's Got a Scoop!* New York: Simon and Schuster, 1992.

Chapter Seven

Amelia Earhart

(1897–1937)

Earhart Takes Flight

BACKGROUND

Amelia Earhart broke boundaries for women in aviation. Born in 1897 in Atchison, Kansas, her adventurous spirit led her to a career in flying. She set many records, lectured on flying, and wrote several books. Her most well-known work, *20 Hrs., 40 Min.,* documents the trip she made in *Friendship,* her first flight across the Atlantic Ocean. Amelia worked for Transcontinental Air Transport, later known as TWA.

She played an instrumental part in aviation history and traveled the world, advocating for the establishment of scheduled passenger flights. In 1937, she attempted to fly around the world. Her plane vanished and she was never found. Years of investigations followed her disappearance, but the mystery remains unsolved.

This play depicts her early childhood and ends when she takes the *Friendship* flight in 1928, her first flight across the Atlantic Ocean.

PRESENTATION SUGGESTIONS

In this script, several characters are on stage for a short time. In order to accommodate these rapid changes, students may enter one or two lines before their own lines are to be delivered. Or, consider reading the script in a circle before using a stage. Students may have suggestions on how to stage the various scenes.

If you choose to perform this play for an audience, backdrops may consist of various planes, or a large map showing the various routes Amelia Earhart flew over her lifetime. For example, a large map of the route the *Friendship* flew may be an appropriate background.

PROPS (OPTIONAL)

1. Hammer and nails
2. Bandage for Pilot #1

LIST OF CHARACTERS

1. Amelia Earhart, *aviator, nickname Millie*
2. Muriel Earhart, *Amelia's younger sister (2½ years younger), nickname Pidge*
3. James Alfred Otis, *Grandfather*

4. Amelia Harres Otis, *Grandmother*

5. Pilot #1, *pilot injured in World War I*

6. Edwin Earhart, *Father*

7. Anita "Neta" Snook, *Amelia's flying instructor*

8. Amy Earhart, *Mother*

9. Louisa, *a student*

10. Min, *a student*

11. Sean, *a student*

12. Marion Perkins, *Director of Denison House*

13. Secretary, *at Denison House*

14. Captain Hilton H. Raily, *Publicist for Putnam Publishers, assisted in organizing Friendship flight*

15. Wilmer Stultz, *Pilot for Friendship flight*

16. Louis "Slim" Gordon, *Mechanic for Friendship flight*

17. Louis Gower, *alternate pilot*

18. Workman #1, *on the shore of Southern Wales*

19. Workman #2, *on the shore of Southern Wales*

Optional:

Additional soldiers in the hospital

Additional students in Amelia's classroom in the Dennison House

‖ EARHART TAKES FLIGHT ‖

Scene One
Setting: Grandparents home in Atchison, Kansas.

Narrator 1: Amelia Earhart was born in 1897 in Atchison, Kansas. She and her younger sister, Muriel, spent a lot of time with their grandparents.

Narrator 2: Amelia liked adventure from the time she was very young. She and Muriel created all sorts of adventures together. Muriel's nickname was Pidge.

Amelia: Pidge, it's a great idea.

Muriel: I don't think so, Millie. We could get into trouble. Especially with Grandma Otis. She's already mad at you for jumping over the gate all the time.

Amelia: We won't get into any trouble. And I like jumping over the gate.

Muriel: Grandma says it's not ladylike, Millie. Only boys jump over gates and fences.

Amelia: Oh, I know what she says. But it's a lot more fun to jump over the gate than just open it and walk through it. Anyone can open a gate and walk through it. How many girls do you know jump over gates, Pidge?

Muriel: You're the only girl I know of that jumps over fences, Millie.

Amelia: And besides, why should boys have all the fun? I'll teach you how to jump over the gate, little sis—if you want to learn.

Muriel: No, thank you.

Amelia: Okay, then help me build this roller coaster. Please?

Narrator 1: Amelia picked up the hammer and nails and waved them at Muriel.

Amelia: Won't you do this with me? It would be really hard to build a roller coaster without you.

Muriel: I don't know.

Amelia: You don't have to ride it if you don't want to, Pidge. Just help me build it.

Muriel: Okay, Millie. I'll help.

Narrator 2: Muriel and Amelia spent the day gathering the wood, hammer, and nails. They needed more help than they realized so Grandpa Otis helped. He measured, cut the wood, and hammered the boards together.

Grandpa: You girls ought to be careful riding this roller coaster. It's as safe as we can make it.

Amelia: It's a wonderful roller coaster, Grandpa. Thank you.

Muriel: It rolls up and down three times.

Grandpa: Okay, so who wants to take the first ride?

Amelia: I do!

Grandpa: Okay, just a few more nails and I think it's all set.

Narrator 1: Amelia's cart made it over the first bump, and then flipped over onto the grass. Grandmother Otis hovered over her.

Grandma Otis: I told you girls to be more careful. James, I would expect you to have better judgment. After all, you are a judge. These two are running around like a couple of boys.

Grandpa: Oh now, they're just having some fun. There's nothing wrong with that. And my judgment here is just as good as in the courtroom. Besides, Millie's not hurt, are you?

Narrator 2: A smile broadened across Amelia's face as she wiped the dirt off her clothes.

Amelia: No, I'm not hurt Grandpa. I can do anything boys can, Grandma. I don't see why they get to have all the fun. And I think I'm going to try that roller coaster again. It felt like I was flying.

Scene Two
Setting: Muriel's room at school.

Narrator 1: Twenty years passed since Amelia's first ride on that roller coaster. Both sisters were in school in different cities. While Muriel was clear on what she wanted to do, Amelia remained unclear.

Narrator 2: In December 1917, Amelia took a break from her studies at Ogontz school and visited her sister at school in Toronto, Canada.

Muriel: I'm so glad you could visit.

Amelia: Me too, Pidge. How's school?

Muriel: It's fine. I plan on being a teacher.

Amelia: Really?

Muriel: And you, what do you want to be?

Amelia: I'm not sure. Ogontz is a good school. I like my roommate, Eleanor. But I just don't know what I want to be.

Muriel: No idea at all?

Amelia: Not really.

Muriel: What about studying medicine, or something along those lines? You would be so good at that.

Amelia: You really think so?

Narrator 2: Amelia looked out the window of Muriel's room. She saw a man on crutches with one leg. She drew in a breath of surprise at the sight.

Amelia: That man on the street. He has just one leg.

Muriel: You can thank the war for that. I hear thousands of men are losing their lives in Europe, many Canadian soldiers as well.

Amelia: Are many like him?

Muriel: I would assume so. There's a hospital nearby and they are always in need of help.

Amelia: Then, that's what I'll do.

Muriel: What will you do?

Amelia: Work at the hospital.

Muriel: Millie, you haven't finished school yet.

Amelia: I can go back later; this is more important.

Narrator 2: Amelia's sense of adventure matched her sense of compassion. She went to work as a nurse in Toronto, Canada, at Spadina Military Hospital.

Narrator 1: She enjoyed serving as a nurse during World War I. She especially liked hearing the stories from the pilots.

Pilot #1: It was incredible up there. We were all flying in alignment and could see the ocean miles below.

Amelia: What was it like being in the sky?

Pilot #1: Amazing. The sky is endless, and I felt like flying forever. It's so peaceful up there.

Amelia: I imagine it would be.

Pilot #1: You should visit the airfields. They're not far away. You can watch the planes take test runs.

Amelia: Can I fly in one?

Pilot #1: 'fraid not. It's a military plane, and only military personnel can fly in them.

Narrator 2: Muriel and Amelia visited the airfields together.

Amelia: Look, Pidge. How amazing would that be? To fly?

Muriel: It looks pretty dangerous to me. There's hardly any room to sit in the plane. There are too many things that can go wrong.

Amelia: You're such a pessimist. Look at all the things that can go right. Up there. You're seeing things from a perspective no one else has seen. Imagine how fast you can get from place to place if you could fly instead of take the train.

Muriel: You're daydreaming again, Millie.

Amelia: I don't think so. You'll see. Flying will be a big part of the very near future.

Muriel: We'll see.

Scene Three
Setting: An airshow.

Narrator 2: After serving as a nurse, Amelia became interested in medicine. She attended Columbia University in New York to pursue this field.

Narrator 1: In 1920, she decided to leave college for a break and visit her parents in Los Angeles, California. She went to an air show with her father.

Edwin: I'm glad you could take a break from your studies.

Amelia: I plan to go back. I just wanted to visit you and mom. It's been too long since I've seen you both. Besides, I'm not entirely sure I want to be a doctor. I need a little time to think about it more before spending more time and money on school.

Edwin: That makes perfect sense to me. Have you been to an air show before?

Amelia: When I was a nurse in Toronto, I used to watch the Canadian pilots fly in the airfields. Other than that, no.

Edwin: You're in for a real treat. From what I understand, the very first flying show was in France in 1909.

Amelia: Really?

Edwin: Yep, in 1909 Louis Bleriot flew across the English Channel. It became known as the first air show.

Amelia: Hey look. They're offering flights for $10. Do you have $10 I can borrow? Promise to pay it back.

Edwin: Sure, have a good time.

Amelia: I plan to. Thanks, Dad.

Narrator 2: After her first flight, Amelia was hooked on flying. She signed up for flying lessons the very next day. Her instructor was Anita Snook, known as Neta.

Narrator 1: Neta was the first woman to graduate from the Curtiss School of Aviation.

Neta: I'm Neta, Neta Snook, your flying instructor.

Amelia: Nice to meet you. Where do we begin?

Neta: First I'll show you the basics and then we'll go up for a short flight. If you look in here, this is called the cockpit. You've got the instrument panel, foot pedals to control the rudder, and yolk. It may all look quite overwhelming, but you'll be learning the use of everything in no time.

Narrator 1: Neta was Amelia's instructor for years to come. Amelia loved nothing more than to be in the air. She worked several part-time jobs to pay for her flying lessons and saved up to buy her own plane.

Narrator 2: Her first plane was a little bright yellow plane that she named Canary. It had 60 horsepower, an air-cooled engine, and was so light that Amelia could pick it up by the tail and move it. She proudly showed it to Neta.

Neta: That's a great little plane, Amelia.

Amelia: Thanks, Neta.

Neta: Let's give it a spin and see how it does.

Amelia: Let's go.

Narrator 1: Amelia and Neta took Canary into the air.

Neta: Amelia, did you check everything out before we got into the air?

Amelia: Sure, why?

Neta: Because one of the engines just stalled. We better land this plane, fast.

Narrator 1: Amelia and Neta landed the plane into a cabbage patch field.

Neta: Amelia, are you hurt?

Amelia: No, you?

Neta: Amelia, always anticipate problems. Check everything before you take Canary up into the air. Okay?

Amelia: Right, sorry.

Neta: Why don't we see about you flying solo? Just promise to check everything out before taking the plane up.

Amelia: Of course, Neta. I think I've learned my lesson.

Narrator 1: In 1922, Amelia broke the height record for women's flying. She flew 14,000 feet. By 1923, she qualified for a pilot's license.

Neta: Congratulations, Amelia.

Amelia: Thanks, Neta. I couldn't have done it without my lessons with you. I finally have my own pilot's license.

Neta: I know. And you're the sixteenth woman to receive it. You should feel great.

Amelia: I do!

Narrator 2: In 1924, Amelia and her mother drove to visit Muriel in Medford, Massachusetts. Amelia sold her plane and bought a sporty convertible car she named the Yellow Peril.

Narrator 1: When they arrived, Muriel was excited to see them both.

Muriel: You're here. Finally. Mom, how are you?

Amy: Fine, thank you. Thank you for having us stay with you.

Muriel: Of course! Millie, how was the drive?

Amelia: Fine, but not as good as flying.

Muriel: Always flying. I'll start calling you flying Millie.

Amelia: You could, now that I have my pilot's license.

Muriel: Congratulations!

Amy: How's teaching junior high treating you, Muriel?

Muriel: Just fine. A bit challenging, but fine.

Amelia: Still teaching English?

Muriel: Of course. And, what will you do here, Millie?

Amelia: Find the nearest airfield immediately.

Muriel: Always flying, aren't you?

Amelia: Mark my words, Pidge. Flying will replace cars and trains one day. Someday everyone will fly.

Scene Four
Setting: Denison House, Amelia's classroom.

Narrator 1: Amelia continued to fly, but she also realized she needed to earn a living. She took a job at the Denison House where she taught English to foreign children. By 1928, she had been teaching there for several years.

Amelia: Today, we're going to study the sky. Everyone get out your paper and pencil.

Louisa: Ms. Earhart?

Amelia: Yes, Louisa.

Louisa: I would like to hear more stories about flying.

Amelia: After the lesson.

Min: Ms. Earhart?

Amelia: Yes, Min.

Min: I agree with Louisa. I would like to hear more stories too. Could you tell us some of the story before we do the lesson?

Sean: Please, Ms. Earhart?

Amelia: I suppose, just one story. I once had a great little plane named Canary. She was perfect. I named her Canary because she was yellow like a canary bird. Canary and I flew over fields, houses, and had so much fun we didn't want to come down.

Narrator 2: Before Amelia could finish her story, Marion Perkins came into the classroom. She was the director of the Denison House.

Marion: Amelia, you have an urgent phone call in the office.

Amelia: Urgent call? I really can't just leave my class unless it's absolutely critical I take it.

Marion: Believe me, Amelia, this is absolutely critical. Go take this call.

Amelia: Excuse me class. Marion, would you please stay with them? We were just about to study the sky.

Marion: Of course. Go take your phone call.

Narrator 2: She rushed to the phone in the office. The secretary sat by the phone.

Secretary: Ms. Earhart. There's a Captain H. H. Raily on the phone for you.

Amelia: Thank you.

Narrator 2: Amelia took the phone. She had never heard of Captain H. H. Raily.

Amelia: Hello?

Raily: Amelia Earhart?

Amelia: Yes.

Raily: How would you like to be the first woman to fly across the Atlantic Ocean?

Amelia: Excuse me?

Raily: We want you to be the first woman to fly across the Atlantic Ocean. There's going to be a flight with Wilmer Stultz. He'll be the pilot. Louis Gower would be the alternate pilot. Louis Gordon is the mechanic. You are the captain of the flight. You would be the first woman to ever fly across the Atlantic Ocean.

Narrator 1: Amelia could hardly believe her ears. Just last year, Charles Lindbergh had done the very same flight. Except he flew solo across the Atlantic. No woman had ever flown over the seas.

Raily: Well Ms. Earhart, what do you say?

Amelia: How could I refuse such an adventure? When do I leave?

Scene Five
Setting: Boston Harbor.

Narrator 2: The crew for the flight were eager to take flight. In June 1928, their adventure began.

Captain Raily: Amelia, this is Bill, Louis Gower, and Louis Gordon. Everyone, meet your captain—Amelia Earhart.

Louis Gordon: You can just call me Slim.

Amelia: Okay, Slim.

Bill: You look like you could be Charles Lindbergh's sister. Did anyone ever tell you that?

Louis Gower: You know, you're right Bill. You do look like Lindbergh's sister.

Slim: Should we call you Lady Lindy?

Amelia: That's catchy. I'm sure the reporters will pick it up.

Raily: Okay, are you ready to take off?

Amelia: Let's go.

Narrator 1: The seaplane *Friendship* sat in the Boston Harbor waiting for its passengers to board. Its golden wings spread seventy-two feet. Its body was bright red orange.

Narrator 2: Sadie Ross, a tugboat, carried the crew to *Friendship*. They climbed into the small plane.

Bill: I've got the controls set up. Everyone get ready for takeoff.

Narrator 1: As the plane took off, Amelia took pictures of the Boston Harbor.

Amelia: I've never been able to see all of Boston like this. I hope these photographs come out!

Slim: I'm sure they will.

Amelia: The spring lock on the cabin door doesn't look very safe. Slim, did you check this out?

Narrator 2: Before Slim could answer, the door swung open. Amelia caught it and held it closed.

Amelia: Well, this is an exciting beginning to our trip! Slim, think you could fix this so we don't fall out?

Slim: Very funny, Lady Lindy. No one's falling out of this craft on my watch.

Louis G.: Let's hope that's the least of our problems. How long is this flight, anyway?

Bill: We are heading to Trepassey first, in Newfoundland. From there, we'll fuel up and take off toward England!

Amelia: Look below, I can see fifteen fishing vessels.

Slim: Bet they can't see each other.

Narrator 2: On June 5th, they landed in Trepassey, Newfoundland. After several days of waiting for bad weather to pass, they refueled to head for England.

Narrator 1: On June 17th, at last it seemed the weather was clear enough for them to take flight. The crew entered *Friendship* once again.

Bill: It won't take off, there's too much weight. We have more fuel on board this time, it's making the plane too heavy to take off.

Amelia: What should we do?

Narrator 2: Louis Gower stepped off the plane.

Louis: Try it now.

Bill: Hey, that did it. We can take off now.

Louis: Guess I'm not. You all go on without me.

Narrator 2: So the three remaining crew members completed the flight. The plane lifted off the waves and climbed once again into the sky.

Amelia: Look at the ocean, the ripples look like an elephant's back.

Bill: You have quite the imagination, Lady Lindy.

Narrator 1: Amelia wrote down everything she saw in her journal.

Amelia: Being up here is like gulping beauty.

Slim: Very poetic.

Narrator 1: It had been 20 hours and 40 minutes since they left Trepassey. Bill landed the plane in the water near some land.

Narrator 2: Some men working on the shore looked up and watched the plane land. Amelia poked her head out of the plane and waved a towel at them.

Workman #1: Do you see that plane?

Workman #2: Yes, looks like they're waving at us. Wave back.

Narrator 1: Both men waved back at the plane. Amelia shouted at them.

Amelia: We've come from America. Where are we?

Workman #1: You are in Burry Port, in Southern Wales.

Bill: We made it!

Slim: Well, Lady Lindy. We've arrived.

Amelia: It was a great flight. *Friendship* is only my first flight. You know I'm going to have to do this more often.

Slim: Somehow, I don't doubt that, Lady Lindy.

Epilogue

Narrator 1: Amelia wrote *20 Hrs., 40 Mins.* about her flight on *Friendship*.

Narrator 2: She went on to write many articles, lecture about flying, and to generate support for scheduled passenger flights.

Narrator 1: She set the record for the fastest nonstop transcontinental flight at 19 hours and 5 minutes.

Narrator 2: In 1935, she became the first person to fly over the Pacific Ocean from Hawaii to California.

Narrator 1: In 1937, she disappeared in her attempt to fly around the world.

Narrator 2: Her disappearance became one of the most famous unsolved mysteries.

FOLLOW-UP ACTIVITIES

Students may create a map that tracks the route of Amelia's flight on *Friendship*, her transcontinental flight, and/or her final flight. This may be a group activity or an individual homework assignment.

For Situation Improv, students may choose to act out situations such as:

- Amelia lecturing to a group of business people on why flying will become the transportation of the future
- Amelia teaching a class on how to fly
- Amelia in 2002, in an airport for the first time

In groups, students may become investigators and create theories on how/why Amelia disappeared in her last flight. They may then present their theories to each other. There are several existing theories discussed in biographies of Amelia Earhart as to why she disappeared. The investigation may serve as an activity to build research skills, as well as teamwork.

REFERENCES

Backus, Jean L. *Letters from Amelia, 1901–1937*. Boston, MA: Beacon Press, 1982.

Davies, Kathleen. *Amelia Earhart Flies Around the World*. New York: Dillon Press, 1994.

Earhart, Amelia. *20 Hrs., 40 Mins.: Our Flight in the Friendship*. New York: G.P. Putnam Sons, 1928.

Langley, Andrew. *Amelia Earhart*. New York: Oxford Press, 1997.

Morey, Eileen. *The Importance of Amelia Earhart*. San Diego, CA: Lucent Books, 1995.

Morrissey, Muriel Earhart, and Carol L. Osborne. *Amelia, My Courageous Sister*. Santa Clara, CA: Osborne, 1987.

Chapter Eight

Laura Ingalls Wilder
(1867–1957)

Growing up a Pioneer

BACKGROUND

The Little House books immortalized Laura Ingalls Wilder's pioneer experiences. When Wilder was growing up, people traveled from place to place by train or covered wagon. The West was becoming increasingly populated as people claimed their homesteads in the western United States. As Laura grew up, she watched the United States change as covered wagons were replaced by cars and airplanes.

At the age of sixty, Laura began writing the now famous Little House books to share her experiences as a pioneer with her daughter, Rose. She wanted to capture the life of a pioneer, a way of life that was now obsolete. Because children wrote Laura asking for more books about her life, she wrote a series of Little House books. The Little House books include:

1. *Little House in the Big Woods*

2. *Little House on the Prairie*

3. *Farmer Boy*

4. *On the Banks of Plum Creek*

5. *By the Shores of Silver Lake*

6. *The Long Winter*

7. *Little Town on the Prairie*

8. *These Happy Golden Years*

9. *The First Four Years*

This play depicts Laura's early childhood (1870s) through settling in De Smet, South Dakota (1879).

PRESENTATION SUGGESTIONS

Laura should be center stage for this reading. The narrators may stand on either side of the stage and remain on stage the entire time. Characters who enter and exit the stage should stand next to Laura. If more than two characters are to come on stage, you may consider having them stand on either side of Laura.

A backdrop may include illustrations that depict pioneer life, such as covered wagons, a prairie land, and/or horses.

PROPS (OPTIONAL)

1. Aprons
2. Bonnets
3. Quilt
4. Suitcases for when they're traveling
5. Fiddle

LIST OF CHARACTERS

1. Narrator 1
2. Narrator 2
3. Laura
4. Mary, *Laura's sister*
5. Ma, *Laura's mother*
6. Pa, *Laura's father*
7. Carrie, *sister*
8. Indian #1
9. Indian #2
10. Gustaf Gustafson, *bought and sold the Ingalls Wisconsin home*
11. Clarence, *a neighbor in Wisconsin*
12. Eva, *a neighbor in Wisconsin*
13. Teacher, *at schoolhouse*
14. Nettie Kennedy, *a classmate in Walnut Grove, Minnesota*
15. Nellie Owens, *a classmate in Walnut Grove, Minnesota*
16. Traveler
17. Johnny Steadman, *worked with the Ingalls at the Burr Oak Hotel*
18. Reuben Steadman, *worked with the Ingalls at the Burr Oak Hotel*
19. Aunt Ladocia

Optional:
Children in the classroom for Scene Three

‖ GROWING UP A PIONEER ‖

Scene One
Setting: Ingalls home in Kansas.

Narrator 1: It was the 1870s. A time before airplanes, automobiles, telephones, computers, television, and yes, even the Internet.

Narrator 2: People who traveled west by covered wagons were pioneers. They were an adventurous lot, seeking out new lands to call their home.

Narrator 1: The Ingalls family included Laura, her older sister Mary, and their parents Caroline and Charles. They had just finished building their home on a prairie in Kansas.

Pa: Here it is, our little house on the prairie. Thank goodness for homesteading!

Laura: For what?

Pa: It's that new law that passed, half pint.

Laura: What law?

Pa: The government wants more people to move and settle out west. The law says all we have to do is live and work on a piece of land for five years. After the five years, the government will give me a deed saying the land belongs to me.

Laura: After five years, we'll own this land?

Ma: That's right.

Laura: Mary, let's go outside and explore in *our* new yard.

Ma: Be back in time to help with dinner, you two.

Mary: We will, Ma. C'mon Laura.

Laura: Hey, I didn't see this trail before. Where do you think it goes?

Mary: I don't know. We'll get in trouble if we follow it, you know we will.

Laura: C'mon Mary, where is your sense of adventure? Let's just follow it for a little while.

Narrator 2: They walked for quite a while on the trail. Mary nudged Laura.

Mary: Laura, I don't think we should be on this trail. There are two Indians up ahead.

Laura: They don't look really happy to see us.

Mary: I bet this is their trail.

Laura: We'd better go home and tell Pa.

Narrator 1: The Indians watched the two girls as they turned away. Breathlessly, Laura and Mary burst into their home.

Laura: Pa! There's an Indian trail going through our farm.

Pa: Slow down, half pint.

Mary: We were on the trail and saw two Indians. They didn't look very happy to see us.

Pa: Indians? Let's just wait and see. I'm sure it's fine.

Narrator 2: The next day, a neighbor paid a visit to the Ingalls home.

Neighbor: Mr. Ingalls, I live a few miles from you. I'm traveling to all the settlers on this land to warn them.

Pa: Warn us about what?

Neighbor: This land is actually Indian territory. Homesteading just isn't as simple as it ought to be, is it? I think records got mixed up, because this land belongs to the Osage Indians.

Pa: Then, we can't stay here. Much obliged for your trouble coming out and telling us.

Neighbor: All right then. Have a nice day.

Pa: You do the same.

Ma: I don't know if it's a good idea to remain here if it's Indian territory.

Pa: I agree. We don't want to make any trouble here. Besides, there is plenty of land out here to claim as our own. We don't need to try to settle on Indian territory.

Ma: I am glad you see it that way!

Pa: Laura. Mary. Start packing, we're leaving Kansas.

Narrator 1: The Ingalls family packed up their belongings in their covered wagon and returned to where they had started, the little house in the big woods of Wisconsin.

Scene Two
Setting: Pepin, Wisconsin.

Narrator 1: Pa met with Gustaf Gustafson, the man who had bought their home in Pepin, Wisconsin.

Gustaf: I need to leave this area for I am unable to make the payments on the home I bought from you.

Pa: We could take it back.

Gustaf: That would be fine. When can you move in?

Pa: Right away!

Narrator 2: The Ingalls family moved back into their home. While they were gone, a new family, the Huelatts, moved into a home a mile down the road. They also had two children, Clarence and Eva.

Narrator 1: All four children liked to spend time together by the creek.

Laura: Clarence, I dare you to go into the creek.

Eva: It's freezing this time of year, Clarence. Don't do it! Besides, Ma will be really angry with you.

Mary: Laura, that's not a fair dare.

Laura: Oh no? You're just chicken, Mary. You would never do anything "wrong."

Mary: Stop it, Laura, you're being childish.

Laura: I *am* a child. Hey look, there's a frog. Bet I can catch it.

Clarence: Bet I can catch it first!

Narrator 1: Clarence and Laura jumped into the shallow creek trying to capture the little frog.

Mary: Laura, get out of that dirty creek right now! You're ruining your dress.

Laura: I almost got 'im.

Clarence: No way, I've almost got him.

Eva: Clarence, please come out of there!

Narrator 2: Laura reached for the frog, tripped on a rock, and fell into the creek. As she fell, she bumped into Clarence, knocking him down as well. They both laughed.

Mary: Now you've done it Laura.

Laura: Done what? It's just creek water.

Clarence: Hey, there goes the frog!

Scene Three
Setting: Ingalls home in Wisconsin.

Narrator 1: Pa asked the family to gather around the small fireplace. He had some news to share.

Pa: There are many people coming to settle here. Too many! So, your ma and I have decided we will move to Minnesota.

Narrator 2: In 1874, the Ingalls family packed their belongings into their covered wagon and moved to Walnut Grove, Minnesota. They also had a new addition to the family, a daughter named Carrie.

Pa: This farm along Plum Creek will be just fine.

Ma: There are plenty of fields with golden wheat we can harvest. Mary and Laura, you will start school. Laura, you're already seven years old! You should be learning how to read and write.

Laura: School?

Mary: Great! When do we start?

Ma: I think tomorrow. The schoolhouse is walking distance from here.

Narrator 2: The next day, Laura and Mary went to school. Their teacher asked the girls to introduce themselves.

Teacher: Class, we have two new students here. Girls, will you please introduce yourselves.

Laura: My name is Laura Ingalls. I am seven years old and we moved here from Wisconsin.

Nellie: Gee, no surprise that you're a country girl.

Teacher: Nellie Owens, please keep your thoughts to yourself.

Nellie: Sorry ma'am.

Mary: I'm Mary, Laura's older sister.

Teacher: Welcome to our class. Boys sit on the right side of the room, and girls sit on the left.

Narrator 2: Their first day of school went well. When school was over, all of the children left the one-room schoolhouse to play outside.

Nettie: My name is Nettie Kennedy. Welcome to Walnut Grove.

Laura: Thanks. Who's the brat that called me a country girl?

Nettie: Nellie Owens. She's from New York and thinks she owns the world.

Laura: Has anyone broken the news to her she doesn't?

Nettie: I don't know if anyone has tried.

Scene Four
Setting: Near their home in Plum Creek.

Narrator 2: Laura, Mary, and Carrie picked wildflowers near their home.

Mary: Carrie, you pick red flowers, and I'll pick the white ones. We can make a red and white bouquet.

Carrie: Okay, Mary.

Laura: I'll pick the yellow ones. Carrie, when you're old enough you can come to school with us.

Carrie: Okay. There's a hopping animal in the flowers.

Laura: What? I don't see anything.

Mary: Let me see.

Carrie: Again, there's more hopping animals.

Laura: Grasshoppers.

Mary: Don't grasshoppers eat wheat?

Laura: Oh no! Do they?

Narrator 2: The Ingalls girls hurried home. Ma was sewing a quilt and pa was putting new strings on his fiddle.

Laura: Pa, we saw grasshoppers in the fields.

Pa: Where, half pint?

Mary: Near the creek.

Ma: Don't worry, girls. I'm sure it's fine.

Narrator 2: But it wasn't fine. The grasshoppers ate all of the wheat and destroyed the crops for many farmers in Walnut Grove.

Narrator 1: There were so many grasshoppers, the girls couldn't walk to school. Pa left home and tried to find work in other towns, but after many months he returned.

Pa: Well, it seems this area has become grasshopper country. There's no work and our farm is destroyed.

Ma: I'll pack the wagon. Where are we going to move to this time?

Pa: Burr Oak in Iowa. We're going to run a hotel with another family, the Steadmans. I met them when I was traveling and looking for work. They invited us to run the Burr Oak Hotel with them.

Scene Five
Setting: Burr Oak Hotel in Burr Oak, Iowa.

Narrator 1: The Burr Oak Hotel was a bustling and busy place. Although Burr Oak was a small town, travelers frequently stopped here to rest. The hotel had eleven rooms and a dining area.

Narrator 2: One night, a traveler entered the lobby looking for a room.

Traveler #1: How much for a room?

Pa: It's twenty-five cents a night. Meals in the dining area are the same price.

Traveler #1: Great, I would like a room for tonight. I'm on my way to Wisconsin.

Pa: We lived there for a while.

Traveler #1: Really? It's getting real crowded back east, so I thought I'd try somewhere west.

Pa: Wisconsin is full of open land. You'll enjoy it.

Traveler #1: Thank you much.

Pa: You're welcome.

Laura: Dinner's at six P.M., sir.

Traveler #1: Thank you, ma'am.

Narrator 2: When they weren't tending to their studies or helping in the hotel, Mary and Laura spent time with Johnny and Reuben, the Steadman boys.

Johnny: There's nothing to do in this town.

Laura: I miss the Prairie.

Mary: More and more people are moving west. Soon, it will be just as crowded as the East. Even the Prairie.

Reuben: Have you been east?

Mary: No.

Reuben: Then how would you know?

Mary: I've just heard.

Johnny: If you miss the Prairie, why don't you move back?

Laura: We left because grasshoppers ate all of the crops. There was no work, so we had to leave.

Johnny: You've been here for a while now, maybe it's changed.

Narrator 1: After two years in Burr Oak, the Ingalls missed Walnut Grove. Although they didn't know if there was work, they decided to take the risk and move back.

Scene Six
Setting: Home in Walnut Grove.

Narrator 2: In 1879, Mary had a long case of the measles, which left her blind. Laura became her sister's eyes, telling her everything she saw and helping with her studies.

Narrator 1: Their aunt, Ladocia, came to visit from the Dakota territory.

Aunt Ladocia: Charles, have you been able to find steady work here?

Pa: No, it's getting very difficult. The farming still hasn't improved much over the last few years. How are you and Hiram doing in the Dakota Territory?

Aunt Ladocia: We're great. In fact, he is working at a railroad camp. He was just saying he needs someone to be a bookkeeper and timekeeper for the employees. Why don't you move out there and take the job?

Pa: Dakota Territory? What do you think, Caroline?

Ma: Charles, if we move one more time, it's the last time. I don't want to keep packing and unpacking our belongings every year or two.

Pa: Done. It will be our last move. Off to the Dakota Territory!

Laura: We're moving again!

Pa: That's right, half pint. One last move, my pioneer girl!

Narrator 2: For the last time, the Ingalls packed their belongings in the covered wagon and traveled to another region of the states. They settled in what is now De Smet, South Dakota.

Epilogue

Narrator 1: When Laura was fifteen, she became a teacher and taught in schools around De Smet for three years.

Narrator 2: On August 25, 1885, she married a farmer Almanzo Wilder. The next year, in 1886, their daughter Rose was born.

Narrator 1: They moved around to many places and settled in Mansfield, Missouri, in the 1890s. As the years went by, Laura saw covered wagons being replaced with automobiles and planes. At the age of sixty, she decided to write down her memories as a pioneer so people could remember what life was like during those times.

Narrator 2: Her first book, *Little House in the Big Woods*, was published in 1932. She received letters from children asking for more of her pioneer stories. She wrote more Little House books over the next several years until there was a total of eight books in the series.

Narrator 1: Laura's books brought pioneer days to life. She died in 1957, at the age of ninety.

FOLLOW-UP ACTIVITIES

The pioneer era is a wonderful theme for students to apply improvisational theatre movement activities. Have students help compose a list of activities done during the pioneer era such as:

- Baking bread
- Churning butter
- Putting shoes on horses
- Sewing clothing
- Washing clothing in a washtub

Put each activity on a piece of paper, and put all of the pieces of paper into a bowl or hat. Two students are on stage, and they choose one of the activities from the hat. They improvise a scene based on this activity, using only movement. The audience participates by trying to guess what they are doing.

Another alternative to this follow-up activity is to have students perform these with words, as described in the Situation Improv activity in Chapter Two.

REFERENCES

Anderson, William. *Laura Wilder of Mansfield*. Mansfield, MI: Laura Ingalls Wilder-Rose Wilder Lane Home and Museum, 1968.

Anderson, William, and Dan Andreasen. *Pioneer Girl: The Story of Laura Ingalls Wilder*. New York: Harpercollins Publishers, 1998.

Blair, Gwenda, and Thomas B. Allen. *Laura Ingalls Wilder*. New York: G.P. Putnam's Sons, 1981.

Gif, Patricia Reilly. *Laura Ingalls Wilder: Growing Up in the Little House*. New York: Viking Kestrel, 1987.

Miller, John E. *Becoming Laura Ingalls Wilder: The Woman behind the Legend*. Columbia: University of Missouri Press, 1998.

Wilder, Laura Ingalls. *Little House on the Prairie*. New York: HarperCollins, 1935.

Chapter Nine

Eleanor Roosevelt
(1884–1962)

Eleanor

BACKGROUND

Eleanor Roosevelt was one of the most influential women of her time. In 1884, she was born into a wealthy family in New York City. Her shy and serious manner diminished as she became involved in social work. She taught classes to children in settlement houses. During World War I, she fed wounded soldiers. Her work for equal opportunity, equal rights, and equal justice for all regardless of someone's gender, ethnicity, or economic status became her legacy.

In 1905, she married Franklin Delano Roosevelt who became the governor of New York in 1928, then the president in 1932. Eleanor was a different kind of First Lady in the White House. She wrote a newspaper column "My Day," traveled extensively giving speeches throughout the country, and lobbied for peace and equal rights at every opportunity. The social reform work she accomplished makes her one of the greatest humanitarians in history.

This play depicts Eleanor's life from her childhood (1890s) through when Franklin is struck with polio in 1921.

PRESENTATION SUGGESTIONS

Eleanor Roosevelt should be center stage. The narrators may stand on either side of the stage and remain on stage the entire time. Characters who enter and exit the stage should stand next to Eleanor, whichever side you choose. If more than two characters are to come onstage, you may consider having them stand on either side of Eleanor. For scene six, you may want to have the wounded soldiers sit in chairs.

For a backdrop, you may have students create a mural with the theme of human rights. You can use mural paper and paste it against cardboard boxes. The mural could contain quotes from Eleanor Roosevelt and/or paintings of people from that time period. You could also have students paint scenes that depict the different times in Eleanor's life.

PROPS (OPTIONAL)

1. Two teacups
2. Bag of bread
3. Two coffee cups and coffeepot

LIST OF CHARACTERS

1. Narrator 1
2. Narrator 2
3. Young Eleanor Roosevelt
4. Anna Roosevelt, *Eleanor's mother*
5. Elliot Roosevelt, *Eleanor's father*
6. Ethel, *friend of Anna Roosevelt's*
7. Boy 1
8. Mademoiselle Souvestre, *Headmaster at Allenswood School*
9. Marjorie, *Eleanor's roommate at Allenswood*
10. Mary Hall, *Eleanor's Grandmother*
11. Maud Nathan, *Director of Consumer League*
12. Franklin Roosevelt
13. Sara Roosevelt, *Franklin's mother*
14. Corrine, *Eleanor's student*
15. Lucy, *Corrine's mother*
16. Teddy Roosevelt, *Eleanor's uncle*
17. Anna, *Eleanor and Franklin's daughter (10)*
18. James, *Eleanor and Franklin's eldest son (9)*
19. Elliot, *Eleanor and Franklin's second oldest son (7)*
20. Soldier 1, *wounded soldier in hospital*
21. Soldier 2, *wounded soldier in hospital*
22. Soldier 3, *wounded soldier in hospital*
23. Soldier 4, *wounded soldier in hospital*
24. Narcissa Vanderlip, *Chairman of the League of Women Voters*
25. Louis Howe, *political advisor*

‖ Eleanor ‖

Scene One
Setting: Anna and Elliot Roosevelt's home.

Narrator 1: Anna Roosevelt is entertaining a friend, Ethel, in her New York City home.

Anna: Eleanor is so serious. Hardly says a word. I just don't know how she will fit into society. Elliot and I go to so many social affairs, and here's our only daughter who hardly says a word.

Ethel: I'm sure Eleanor will grow out of it Anna. All children do. You and Elliot are marvelous parents.

Anna: I don't know if Eleanor will. She never smiles.

Narrator 2: Young Eleanor stood in the doorway and quietly watched her mother and guest sip tea.

Ethel: Eleanor, why don't you come in and say hello.

Anna: Come in, Granny.

Ethel: Granny? Why on earth would you call her Granny?

Anna: I told you, she's so serious and solemn. Like a grandmother. Now, come in, Granny, and say a proper hello.

Young Eleanor: Hello, ma'am.

Anna: Now, that wasn't so difficult, was it?

Ethel: Nice to see you, Eleanor. What a lovely dress you are wearing.

Young Eleanor: Thank you.

Narrator 1: Thanksgiving was one of Eleanor's favorite times of year. Her father, Elliot, would take her to the newsboys' clubhouses to help serve Thanksgiving dinner.

Elliot: C'mon Little Nell. Another Thanksgiving has come for us to help others.

Narrator 2: Eleanor looked at the young boys in dirty clothes. Some of them even wore ripped clothing.

Elliot: Look at these boys. It's the late 1890s! Everyone should have enough food and clothing.

Young Eleanor: Why don't they have enough food or clothing, Father?

Elliot: Their families don't have enough money to buy food or clothing. So, they come to places like this house to get help. Places like this house could not exist without the help of people like you and me. Volunteers, that's you and me, Little Nell. We volunteer our time to help others who aren't as lucky.

Boy 1: May I have some bread now?

Narrator 2: Eleanor looked up at her father to see if it was okay.

Elliot: Go ahead.

Narrator 1: Eleanor pulled a piece of bread from the bag and handed it to the young boy.

Boy 1: Thanks.

Eleanor: Where is his home?

Elliot: He may not have one. Some of the poor live in wooden shanties, or empty lots. They sleep anywhere that they can stay warm.

Narrator 2: Eleanor could not believe her ears. Her family was one of the wealthiest in New York City. To have no home, no food, and no money was unimaginable.

Scene Two
Setting: Allenswood, a private school in London, England.

Narrator 1: By the time Eleanor was ten years old, both her parents passed away. She and her younger brother went to live with their grandmother, Mary Hall.

Narrator 2: Eleanor's parents wanted her to study in Europe. Grandmother Hall honored this wish. In September 1899, Eleanor arrived at Allenswood, a private school for girls located outside of London, England.

Marjorie: My name is Marjorie. Looks like we'll be rooming together.

Eleanor: I'm Eleanor, Eleanor Roosevelt.

Marjorie: Come on then. I'll show you around and teach you the rules.

Eleanor: There are rules?

Marjorie: Oh yes, Mademoiselle Souvestre has plenty of rules. Our rooms must be kept neat all day long. There's a schedule for everything you could imagine. Meals, classes, play time—everything is on a schedule.

Eleanor: It sounds strict.

Marjorie: It is. Mademoiselle also wants us to speak French all day. No one really does, but we try.

Narrator 2: Mademoiselle approached Eleanor and Marjorie.

Mademoiselle: Marjorie, thank you so much for showing our new student the grounds. Eleanor Roosevelt, I am Mademoiselle Souvestre.

Eleanor: Bonjour.

Mademoiselle: You speak French?

Eleanor: When I was a young child, my caretaker was French.

Mademoiselle: We shall get along splendidly, ma jeune élève.

Marjorie: What does that mean?

Eleanor: My young student.

Narrator 2: During Eleanor's years at Allenswood, her shyness began to disappear. She loved to learn and made many friends. Her friendship with Mademoiselle Souvestre flourished.

Narrator 1: Eleanor did not go home for the holidays. Instead, she traveled with Mademoiselle around Europe.

Eleanor: Thank you for bringing me to Italy. It is truly beautiful.

Mademoiselle: Eleanor, it is my pleasure to show Europe to you. Eleanor, every one of us has the opportunity to decide how we want to live.

Eleanor: What do you mean?

Mademoiselle: Some people live in fear, never doing, changing, or helping. Others live life, helping, taking action, and making a difference.

Eleanor: That is not a difficult decision. I want to make changes.

Mademoiselle: In the years you have been my student, Eleanor, I have watched you grow into a leader. Be sure to use that skill throughout your life to make changes. Do not let fear hold you back from doing something meaningful with your life.

Eleanor: Thank you, Mademoiselle. I appreciate your kind words.

Narrator 1: After three years at Allenswood, Eleanor returned to the United States. Her experiences at the school and with Mademoiselle had a lasting impact on her.

Scene Three
Setting: Grandmother Hall's home.

Narrator 1: In 1902, Eleanor returned to the United States. She volunteered at the Rivington Settlement House. Her grandmother worried about her.

Grandmother: Eleanor, that neighborhood is dangerous. It's in the slums.

Eleanor: It's not dangerous. It's just people with less money living there, people in need of help. The Settlement House offers programs for the children to take classes and learn. I'm honored to be there.

Grandmother: At least take a private carriage there.

Eleanor: I will travel there as would anyone else—by streetcar.

Grandmother: I don't want you walking through those streets by yourself.

Eleanor: Stop this incessant worrying! The work I do there is wonderful. The children I teach love to learn. Just when I think I'm a terrible teacher, a student takes the time to thank me. I will not stop going.

Narrator 2: In 1903, Eleanor joined the Consumer League. She met with the director of this organization, Maud Nathan.

Maud: We appreciate your help, Eleanor. It's very kind of you to donate your time.

Eleanor: Of course, I'm happy to donate my time. Please tell me more about what you are doing.

Maud: As you know, many women and children work in factories. They work long hours with very little pay. We are working to improve those conditions. We want a better place to work, better pay, and shorter hours.

Eleanor: How long are the hours?

Maud: Sometimes fourteen hours a day, six days a week. Oftentimes the workers only earn six dollars a week.

Eleanor: What can we do?

Maud: Work together, form unions, create laws. We have to join forces to create healthy working conditions for everyone.

Eleanor: Let me know how I can help.

Scene Four
Setting: On the train.

Narrator 1: Eleanor did most of her volunteer work in the city. Occasionally, she took a break and traveled to her grandmother's country home outside of New York City.

Narrator 2: She looked out the window as the train carried her toward her grandmother's country house. She noticed Franklin, a boy she had met at many social occasions.

Eleanor: Franklin? Is that you?

Franklin: Eleanor, how are you?

Eleanor: Franklin, my goodness. It's been a long time. I'm fine. And you?

Franklin: Just fine. Where are you traveling to today?

Eleanor: My grandmother's in Tivoli. And you?

Franklin: My mother's home in Hyde Park. What have you been doing?

Eleanor: I have been doing volunteer work in a number of places. What has been occupying your time?

Franklin: Law school at Harvard. I have also been writing for the *Harvard Crimson*, the school newspaper. Law school is challenging and fascinating.

Eleanor: I would imagine it is.

Franklin: I would like to introduce you to my mother. She's in the next train car.

Eleanor: That sounds lovely.

Narrator 1: Eleanor and Franklin walked to the next train car where Franklin's mother was waiting.

Narrator 2: Franklin's father passed away two years before. His mother still wore all black and a heavy black veil mourning her husband's death. Her morbid appearance surprised Eleanor.

Franklin: Mother, this is Eleanor Roosevelt. Eleanor, my mother, Sara.

Narrator 1: Eleanor wasn't sure how to react to such a grim-looking woman. She decided it was best to be exceedingly polite.

Eleanor: So nice to meet you.

Sara: Yes. Your uncle is president, correct?

Eleanor: Yes, to the world he is President Teddy Roosevelt. To me, he's Uncle Teddy.

Sara: I see.

Narrator 2: Eleanor and Franklin continued to see each other. She invited Franklin to accompany her to visit one of her students who was ill.

Eleanor: She lives in this building.

Franklin: People live in this building?

Eleanor: Yes, Franklin. Do you think everyone has fine china and perfectly polished floors in their homes?

Franklin: Of course not, but this building—it's awful—dirty and depressing.

Eleanor: You can see why so many people need help. Come on now, I promised Corrine I would visit her.

Narrator 2: Eleanor and Franklin entered the small apartment. Corrine's mother, Lucy, greeted them.

Lucy: Thank you for coming, Eleanor. She's been looking forward to your visit all day.

Eleanor: Of course. Franklin, this is Lucy.

Franklin: Nice to meet you.

Lucy: Likewise. Corrine, your teacher is here.

Corrine: Ms. Roosevelt is here? I'm so happy to see you!

Narrator 2: Eleanor sat with Corrine for hours. Reading stories to her and telling her how much the other students missed her.

Eleanor: We should leave now. Corrine, promise you'll rest and get better soon.

Corrine: I promise. Thanks for coming to see me, Ms. Roosevelt.

Eleanor: You're welcome.

Narrator 2: Eleanor and Franklin left the run-down apartment building. Franklin was amazed by Eleanor's capacity for compassion.

Narrator 1: After two more years of spending time together, Franklin asked Eleanor to marry him.

Narrator 2: Eleanor called her Uncle Teddy with the news.

Eleanor: Uncle Teddy, he's a nice person with a good heart. Would you please walk me down the aisle?

Teddy: I would be DEE-lighted! Just one thing, I am a busy man running the country.

Eleanor: Of course.

Teddy: Let me find a date that I have no commitments. I'm afraid I'll have to pick your wedding date, my dear.

Eleanor: Oh, that's fine with us. I'm just grateful you can make the time. We'll see you soon Uncle Teddy.

Teddy: Take care, Eleanor. Your parents would be very happy for you.

Scene Five
Setting: Franklin and Eleanor's home in New York City.

Narrator 1: Eleanor and Franklin were married on March 17, 1905. Between 1906 and 1916, Eleanor and Franklin had six children.

Narrator 2: Franklin had entered a life of politics and in 1913 was appointed the assistant secretary of the Navy by President Woodrow Wilson.

Narrator 1: By 1917, the United States joined World War I. Franklin's job required him to travel to Navy bases all over the world.

Eleanor: This is the first time American troops will be sent overseas since the Spanish-American war in 1898.

Franklin: I realize this.

Eleanor: President Wilson's address to Congress both terrified and inspired me. The Central Powers are literally taking over the world.

Franklin: Germany seems unstoppable. Just two years ago, they sank the British ship *Lusitania.*

Eleanor: That event by itself killed twelve hundred people. I am concerned about sending American soldiers to Europe.

Franklin: We are joining the most powerful defenses in the world. France and Great Britain. With our resources, Germany and Austria-Hungary will not win.

Narrator 2: Anna, James, and Elliot heard their parents discussing the war.

Anna: Father, you are not going to Europe, are you?

Franklin: I might need to. Your mother will stay here with all of you. Don't worry.

Eleanor: Anna, I will need your help taking care of John and Franklin Junior while your father is away.

James: I'm nine years old. I can help.

Elliot: I'm seven. I can help too.

Eleanor: Yes, you can all help. We will all help each other.

Franklin: I need to finish my packing.

Scene Six
Setting: American Red Cross.

Narrator 1: During the war, Eleanor continued her volunteer work. The American Red Cross needed people in the military hospitals to help the wounded soldiers. She served soup to soldiers, cleaned the floors, and offered a compassionate ear to soldiers who needed to talk.

Eleanor: Would you like another bowl of soup?

Soldier 1: No, ma'am. Have you heard any news?

Eleanor: Nothing new, I'm afraid.

Soldier 2: They're calling this war the war to end all wars.

Soldier 3: The Great War.

Eleanor: Let's hope it will be the last war. We should be able to find a way for all countries all over the world to live together, without battles.

Soldier 2: I would like some coffee.

Eleanor: Of course. I'll get some for you. Anyone else?

Soldier 4: I would like some too, ma'am.

Narrator 2: Eleanor poured hot cups of coffee for the wounded soldiers.

Eleanor: Here you are.

Soldier 4: Thank you.

Soldier 2: Thank you, ma'am. What is your name?

Eleanor: Eleanor Roosevelt.

Soldier 3: Eleanor Roosevelt, you are one of the most compassionate people I know. Who else would spend their days talking to a bunch of wounded soldiers?

Soldier 1: I second that. She's been here every day since I was brought in. That was two weeks ago.

Eleanor: Thank you for your kind words, gentlemen. It's not necessary to thank me.

Narrator 1: On November 11, 1918, the Great War came to an end.

Narrator 2: Both the Central Powers and Allies signed the armistice, an agreement for the warring nations to cease fighting and keep peace.

Scene Seven
Setting: Eleanor and Franklin's home.

Narrator 1: For the first time in history, women were granted the right to vote. Eleanor joined the League of Women Voters. She invited the chairman of the New York branch of the League, Narcissa Vanderlip, to her home.

Narcissa: Thank you for inviting me to your home.

Eleanor: I'm glad you could come.

Anna: May I listen?

Narcissa: I would be delighted to have you listen.

Anna: Thank you.

Narcissa: Now that women have the right to vote, we have formed this organization to educate women about the U.S. government.

Eleanor: I appreciate your efforts.

Anna: What are we voting for?

Eleanor: Everything, Anna. We can now vote just like men do. When you get older, you can vote. You now have a voice in what happens to our government, who is elected, and what laws will pass.

Narcissa: Anna, it's an important time for women. Eleanor, I was hoping you would serve on the legislative committee.

Anna: A legi— what?

Narcissa: It's a committee that will look at the process of making laws, Anna.

Eleanor: Some laws pass and some do not. Because women can now vote, we need to know what laws are being considered so women can make an intelligent decision on whether or not to support those laws.

Narcissa: Eleanor, we would like you to report on national laws.

Eleanor: I would be honored.

Scene Eight
Setting: Eleanor and Franklin's home.

Narrator 2: In 1921, the Roosevelt family returned from a family vacation on Campobello Island. Franklin became very sick and was diagnosed with polio.

Narrator 1: No cure existed for polio. Franklin was very weak and lost the use of his legs. Eleanor spent weeks caring for him. One afternoon, Louis Howe came to visit them.

Louis: How is Franklin?

Eleanor: He is weak, Louis. Very weak.

Louis: You know I've been his political advisor for years.

Eleanor: Yes.

Louis: I think he can continue his career in politics, but he will need your help.

Eleanor: I'm listening.

Louis: You could campaign for him. Meeting people, making speeches, traveling, and so on. Eleanor, I know you could do it.

Eleanor: I don't know about that, I get nervous speaking in front of people.

Louis: I could help you. I'll coach you. He could become governor of New York one day, maybe even president of the United States. Think of all the good you could do if you were both in office.

Eleanor: You are right. There are so many things that need changing to help people. I'll talk to Franklin when he awakes. Thank you for visiting, Louis. Perhaps you can come for dinner sometime when Franklin is feeling better.

Narrator 2: Louis left the Roosevelt home. Eleanor went to speak with her husband about his political career.

Eleanor: Your political career isn't over because of this illness Franklin. You can't walk, but you can still think. This country needs you.

Franklin: How will I travel around the country and campaign for office?

Eleanor: I will be your eyes, ears, and legs.

Franklin: Are you sure, Eleanor?

Eleanor: I will do it until you are well again. Louis said he would coach me on how to give speeches. You've already served this country well, I know we can do more.

Franklin: Thank you.

Eleanor: No need to thank me. Some people say that you could become governor of New York someday. I believe them. Others believe you might even be president.

Franklin: That would be something.

Eleanor: We could help many, many people if we were in the White House. I never planned on being a president's wife, but now I see all of the positive outcomes that could bring.

Franklin: You would make a great First Lady.

Eleanor: There are simply too many wrongs to right. I will be your eyes, ears, and legs because being in politics is something I want too, Franklin. As Mademoiselle Souvestre once told me, "help people, take action, and make a difference."

Epilogue

Narrator 1: Eleanor traveled around the country giving speeches and campaigning for her husband.

Narrator 2: In 1928, Franklin became the governor of New York. Eleanor visited prisons, mental hospitals, and other institutions throughout New York. She and Franklin discussed the conditions of these places and how they can be improved.

Narrator 1: In 1932, Franklin and Eleanor moved into the White House. Franklin became the thirty-second president of the United States.

Narrator 2: In 1935, Eleanor began writing a newspaper column, "My Day," where she expressed her opinions of the current affairs in the world.

Narrator 1: When she found out that the Daughters of the American Revolution refused to allow African American singer Marian Anderson to sing at their event, Eleanor promptly terminated her membership to the organization.

Narrator 2: She then arranged a concert at Lincoln Memorial for 75,000 people that featured Marian Anderson.

Narrator 1: She continued to fight for equal human rights long after she left the White House.

Narrator 2: She served in many organizations, including the United Nations for Human Rights, Women's Division of the Democratic State Committee, National Youth Administration, and many more.

Narrator 1: She was known for her energy, compassion, and thirst for life. She herself said, "Life was meant to be lived." She lived a full life to the age of seventy-eight.

FOLLOW-UP ACTIVITIES

Eleanor Roosevelt wrote her newspaper column "My Day" from 1935 until the time she died. Her words inspired many U.S. citizens. An excellent exercise for students to understand Eleanor Roosevelt is to interpret her own words. This journaling exercise allows students to reflect on human rights—their own opinion as well as Eleanor Roosevelt's.

Steps

1. From the list of quotes from Eleanor Roosevelt below, have students choose one quote.

2. Each student should then journal about the quote for 10–15 minutes. They should address the following questions:

   • What does this quote mean to you?
   • What do you think Eleanor Roosevelt meant in this quote?
   • What was happening in the world in the year she wrote this quote?
   • What do you like about this quote?
   • What do you dislike?

3. This activity may also be in small discussion format. Students may divide into groups of three to five and discuss the questions in step 2 for one quote. They can then present their answers with the rest of the class.

Quotes from Eleanor Roosevelt's Column "My Day"

1. "Real prosperity can only come out when everybody prospers" (March 19, 1936).

2. "It seems difficult to make humanity rise to certain heights except in crises" (September 23, 1938).

3. "All wars eventually act as boomerangs and the victor suffers as much as the vanquished" (February 7, 1939).

4. "The things you refuse to meet today always come back at you later on, usually under circumstances which make the decision twice as difficult as it originally was" (July 13, 1939).

5. "So often people you admire at a distance do not mean so much to you after you meet them" (February 12, 1940).

6. "It is our freedom to progress that makes us all want to live and to go on" (May 29, 1941).

7. "How do you explain why communism has any appeal at all to intellectuals or to the intelligent people of countries that are not suffering from great economic distress?" (February 12, 1955).

8. "On January 1, 1963, we will celebrate 100 years of emancipation of the Negro. In other and words, we are near the 100-year mark, and that is a long time—if we really mean to carry out Lincoln's Emancipation Proclamation—to correct the evils of slavery and prove to the world that we really do believe in equality of all human beings" (May 5, 1956).

9. "It is not fair to ask of others what you are not willing to do yourself" (June 15, 1946).[1]

NOTE

1. For additional quotes, refer to: Elmblidge, David. *Eleanor Roosevelt's My Day.* Volume 3. New York: Pharos Books, 1991; Elmblidge, David. *Eleanor Roosevelt's My Day.* Volume 2. New York: Pharos Books, 1990; and Elmblidge, David. *Eleanor Roosevelt's My Day.* Volume 1. New York: Pharos Books, 1989.

REFERENCES

Elmblidge, David. *Eleanor Roosevelt's My Day.* Volume 1. New York: Pharos Books, 1989.

Elmblidge, David. *Eleanor Roosevelt's My Day.* Volume 2. New York: Pharos Books, 1990.

Elmblidge, David. *Eleanor Roosevelt's My Day.* Volume 3. New York: Pharos Books, 1991.

Freedman, Russell. *Eleanor Roosevelt: A Life of Discovery.* New York: Clarion Books, 1993.

Goodsell, Jane. *Eleanor Roosevelt.* New York: Thomas Crowell Company, 1970.

Hacker, Carlotta. *Humanitarians.* New York: Crabtree Publishing Company, 1999.

Morey, Eileen. *The Importance of Eleanor Roosevelt.* San Diego, CA: Lucent Books, 1998.

Parks, Deborah A., and Melva L. Ware. *Eleanor Roosevelt: Freedom's Champion.* Alexandria, VA: Time Life Education, 2000.

Roosevelt, Eleanor. *This I Remember.* New York: Harper and Brothers, 1949.

Chapter Ten

Babe Didrikson Zaharias
(1911–1956)

Babe's Beginnings

BACKGROUND

Voted Woman Athlete of the Year six times by the Associated Press, Babe Didrikson Zaharias is known as one of the most versatile female athletes in American history. Born in Beaumont, Texas, in 1911, Mildred Ella Didrikson was the second youngest of seven children. As a young girl, she repeatedly won competitions in any sport she tried. Neighborhood kids decided she was their home run hero, just like Babe Ruth.

The nickname "Babe" remained with her as she continued to make strides in the world of sports. In the 1930s, professional sports for women did not exist, only opportunities at the amateur level. Babe took every opportunity to win at everything she did. She won Olympic medals in track and field, eighty-two golf tournaments, and mastered many other sports, including swimming, bowling, and tennis. Her self-confidence and determination redefined the world of sports for women.

This play depicts Babe's early childhood (1920s) through her winning gold medals at the 1932 Olympics.

PRESENTATION SUGGESTIONS

Babe should be center stage for this reading. The narrators may stand on either side of the stage and remain on stage the entire time. Characters who enter and exit the stage should stand next to Babe, whichever side you choose. If more than two characters are to come onstage, you may consider having them stand on either side of Babe. For scene three, you may want to have the "baseball plates" face toward the audience, so when Babe hits the home run, all of the characters are watching it go over the audience's heads.

For a backdrop, you may have students create a mural with the theme of sports. You can use butcher paper and paste it against cardboard boxes. The mural could illustrate the timeline of which sports Babe participated in during her lifetime. Alternatively, having various sports equipment on the stage would also be appropriate.

PROPS (OPTIONAL)

1. Stick (to stir soap and water)
2. Bucket
3. Soap
4. Scrub brushes (2)

5. Short pieces of rope (2)

6. Sports page from 1920 Texas newspaper; students may create this

7. Baseball bat

8. Sunglasses for Clark Gable

9. Two gold Olympic medals and one silver for Babe to wear at the end

LIST OF CHARACTERS

1. Narrator 1

2. Narrator 2

3. Mom

4. Dad

Didrikson children, order of age youngest to oldest:

5. Arthur, *nickname Bubba*

6. Mildred (Babe)

7. Lillie

8. Louis

9. Esther

10. Dora

11. Ole, Jr.

Neighborhood children:

12. Milton

13. Sam

14. Morris

If you have a larger class, more students can be in this scene (3)

15. Bea

16. Colonel

17. Jane

18. Carol

19. Olympic Teammate #1

20. Olympic Teammate #2

21. Olympic Teammate #3

22. Clark Gable

BABE'S BEGINNINGS

Scene One
Setting: 1920, Didrikson home in Beaumont, Texas.

Narrator 1: Mildred, later known as Babe, liked a challenge. She was one of seven children. She didn't perform her house chores in the same manner as most kids.

Narrator 2: One of her chores was to wash the porch floor. Her mother gave her scrub brushes, soap, and a bucket of water.

Mother: This porch has been a terrible mess. Mildred, please get it as clean as possible. Mind your little brother too.

Babe: Will do, Mom. Bubba, you just watch your big sister get this porch sparkling clean.

Bubba: That's a lot of porch to clean!

Babe: I know. Hand me that rope, would ya?

Bubba: How will rope help you clean the porch?

Babe: You'll see. Why don't you pour the soap into the bucket for me and mix it up with something.

Bubba: Like what?

Babe: Oh, I don't know. Grab a stick from the yard.

Narrator 2: Bubba mixed the water and soap together as he watched his sister tie a soap brush to her foot.

Bubba: What are you doing now?

Babe: Well, if I have to get this porch as clean as possible, there's more weight if my whole body is on the scrub brushes than if I just use my arms. So, I'm going to skate till this porch sparkles! Spill a little of that soap water, Bubba.

Bubba: I'm spillin' it!

Narrator 1: Bubba tipped the bucket until the water spread over the porch. Babe glided around the floor, laughing.

Babe: This is the way to get a floor clean, Bubba.

Mother: Mildred, such an inventive way to get the floor clean. When you're done, would you please go to the store and get some milk and bread.

Babe: Will do, Mama. That will give me the chance to beat my running time to the store and back.

Arthur: That streetcar has yet to beat you, Mildred.

Babe: I know it. All the people on that streetcar laugh as I run by.

Narrator 2: Bubba continued to spill more of the soapy water on the floor while Mildred skated across the porch.

Scene Two
Setting: 1920, Living room in Didrikson home.

Narrator 2: One of the Didrikson traditions was for Ole, their dad, to read the sports page to his children.

Dad: Okay, everyone, gather 'round. Let's see who is doing what in the world of sports.

Narrator 1: All the children—Ole Jr., Dora, Esther, Lillie, Louis, Mildred, and Bubba—sat around their dad as he opened the newspaper.

Ole Jr.: Anything in there about Babe Ruth, Dad?

Dad: Ole Jr., what can you tell me about Babe Ruth?

Mildred: I know. He is the greatest baseball player to ever live. Hits more home runs than anyone in the world.

Ole Jr.: He asked me, Mildred.

Mildred: You just weren't fast enough.

Dora: Is Mildred in that page yet, Daddy?

Lillie: She should be. You beat all the neighborhood kids in any sport.

Mildred: Of course I do, I practice all the time.

Dad: All successful athletes have to practice—a lot. Look at the Olympics. People train their whole lives just to compete against each other and try to win the gold.

Mildred: Sign me up!

Dad: Well, now Mildred. I suppose you all can achieve anything you set your minds to. Now look at here, Babe Ruth has been sold to another team!

Louis: You're kidding! I thought he'd be with the Boston Red Sox forever.

Dad: Looks like he's joining the New York Yankees.

Esther: The Yankees? They're a lucky team to have him!

Mildred: You just wait, someone will write about me in that sports page one day.

Dad: I have no doubt that's true.

Mom: Okay everyone, wash up for dinner.

Ole Jr.: Babe's going to the Yankees, Mom.

Mom: Is that so?

Dad: You all heard your mom, wash up for dinner.

Narrator 2: All the children headed for the washroom to clean their hands, except Babe.

Babe: Can I look at that paper, Dad?

Dad: Of course.

Babe: I can't believe Babe Ruth left the Red Sox.

Dad: When you're that good, I guess you can love the sport you play and play it for anyone, anywhere.

Babe: Why aren't there any women in these sports pages?

Dad: There are no professional sports teams for women, Mildred.

Babe: Not yet, anyway. Someone *will* write about me one day. You'll see.

Dad: I'm sure they will. But that day isn't here, so why don't you go wash your hands for dinner?

Narrator 1: Babe followed her brothers and sisters to the washroom, with thoughts of being a sports star rolling in her mind.

Scene Three
Setting: 1921, Outside in the sandlot with neighborhood children playing.

Narrator 1: On a summer day, some of the kids from the neighborhood were playing baseball in the sandlot. Babe, Lillie, and Arthur approached them.

Babe: Can we play?

Milton: We don't let girls play.

Mildred: Didn't you hear? The United States is sending a team of women to compete in the swimmers' event. Plus, now women have the right to vote. So girls are playing now in everything, so why shouldn't you let me play?

Milton: Because you're a girl.

Mildred: Are you afraid I might win or something, Milton?

Sam: Have you seen her jump those bushes? She can even run faster than the streetcar. I've seen you with groceries in your arms running faster than the streetcar. C'mon, Milton. Let her play.

Sam: It's no big deal. I think we should let her play too.

Milton: Okay, Mildred. You can play. We only have room for one more player.

Babe: Fine. Lillie and Bubba, you can watch, okay?

Bubba: You hit a home run like Babe Ruth, Mildred.

Babe: I'll do my best!

Narrator 2: Babe picked up the stick that served as a baseball bat. She adjusted her stance and looked at Milton, the pitcher. Sam stood behind her as he put down his catcher's mask and nodded for Milton to throw the pitch.

Narrator 1: The ball slammed into the baseball stick. Babe's arms let the bat go and she stared into the distance.

Sam: Look at that ball go!

Morris: Go? It's completely gone.

Bubba: Go, Mildred!

Lillie: Way to hit it out of the park, just like Babe Ruth.

Milton: Wow! I've never seen a girl or anyone hit like that.

Morris: That's what we'll call you from now on, Babe.

Bubba: Way to go Babe! That ball is out of sight!

Babe: Babe Didrikson. Sounds good to me!

Sam: Babe, you might have hit a home run, but you still have to run the bases.

Babe: Of course, I didn't forget.

Sam: I didn't think so.

Scene Four
Setting: 1930, Didrikson home.

Narrator 1: Babe came home from school with one of her teammates, Bea Smith.

Bea: What are you doing this weekend, Babe?

Babe: Practicing, what else?

Bea: You practice more than anyone I know.

Babe: I'm on every high school women's team at school. That's volleyball, baseball, tennis, swimming, and golf.

Bea: Don't forget basketball.

Babe: Right, the Miss Royal Purples.

Bea: I can't believe you forgot that one! We haven't lost a game since you joined.

Babe: That's why I have to practice all the time. Being good at sports doesn't just happen automatically. I want to be the greatest athlete that ever lived.

Bea: You don't have high ambitions or anything, now do you?

Babe: Quit joking around.

Mom: Hi girls. Babe, did you see the newspaper? They wrote about you again. Here it is.

Bea: Wow! Look at the headlines, Babe. "Beaumont Girl Stars Again." You're famous!

Babe: Just lil' ol' me down here in small Beaumont, Texas. After high school, I want to keep playing.

Bea: Oh, I'm sure you will. One of these days, a talent scout will be at our games watching you.

Mom: I'll bet there have been some there already.

Babe: Think so?

Mom: Sure. Isn't there a game tonight?

Babe: Yes. Look at the time. Bea, we better get back to the gym and warm up.

Bea: You are always practicing.

Babe: I want to win.

Narrator 2: That night, after the game, a man rushed up to Babe.

Colonel: Ms. Didrikson?

Babe: Yep, call me Babe. Everyone else does.

Colonel: Okay then, Babe. My name is Colonel Melvin McCombs. I am with an insurance company, Employers Casualty Insurance. We sponsor a women's basketball team, the Golden Cyclones.

Babe: Really? I'm listening.

Colonel: How would you like to move to Dallas and play on our team?

Babe: Play professionally?

Colonel: It's a semi pro team, but you would be playing for the company. It's a great team and we would sure love to have you.

Babe: Dallas is pretty far away from Beaumont. But, it sounds like a start. I am working toward being the greatest athlete that ever lived.

Colonel: Well then, this would be a start in the right direction.

Babe: Okay, let's hammer out the details and move on with it!

Scene Five
Setting: Spring 1930, First game with the Golden Cyclones.

Narrator 1: Babe and her teammates were getting ready for the game against the Sun Oil Company.

Colonel: Everyone ready for the game?

Babe: You bet.

Jane: We're ready.

Carol: Let's win this one!

Babe: We will win this one. I'm going to be the star forward.

Jane: We already have someone playing that position.

Babe: Well, you have someone new to the position starting now. I am the star forward.

Carol: Who do you think you are?

Babe: The greatest athlete that ever lived.

Jane: She's got some nerve.

Narrator 2: Babe did take over that position. She scored 14 points. She continued to win game after game. The newspaper headlines read "Babe Didrikson Scores 210 Points in 5 Games."

Narrator 1: The teammates were getting annoyed with Babe's overly confident attitude, and the Colonel knew Babe's success would attract scouts from other companies to try and lure her away.

Narrator 2: The Colonel decided to introduce Babe to sports where athletes were recognized for their individual efforts.

Colonel: Babe, I thought you might be interested in trying out some other sport events. I'd like to take you to a track meet.

Babe: Okay, let's go.

Narrator 2: In the spring of 1930, they arrived at a track meet at Southern Methodist University. She saw a javelin lying on the ground.

Babe: What's this?

Colonel: A javelin.

Babe: What do you do with it?

Colonel: It's part of an event in track and field. You hold it over your shoulder, and toss it like a spear. The idea is to see how far you can throw it.

Babe: Why are they throwing that flat ball?

Colonel: That's a discus. It's heavy and the goal of the game is to throw it. Whoever throws it the farthest, wins. I thought you might be interested in some of these track and field events because you can compete in them at the Olympics.

Babe: You want me to train for the Olympics?

Colonel: Why not, Babe? You're one of the most talented athletes I've ever seen, not that you didn't already know that. You could win the gold.

Babe: Could win the gold? I will win the gold. How many events are there in track and field?

Colonel: Nine or ten.

Babe: I'm going to win them all!

Scene Six
Setting: 1932, On the train, on route to the Olympics in Los Angeles, California.

Narrator 1: Over the last two years, Babe trained for all the events in track and field. She was determined to win.

Narrator 2: Babe was one of fifteen women selected for the U.S. Olympic track team. They all took the train together to Los Angeles, California.

Olympic Teammate #1: Let's play cards. It's a long ride from Illinois to California.

Olympic Teammate #2: I have some cards, I'll get them out.

Babe: I'm going to win every single event.

Olympic Teammate #3: You're not overconfident now, are you? What are you doing?

Babe: Stretching my legs. I'm going to run the length of the train.

Olympic Teammate #2: Don't you ever stop training?

Babe: No. That's why I'm going to win.

Narrator 2: They arrived in Los Angeles. Reporters swarmed around Babe. They heard about her incredible versatility in athletics and sheer determination to win.

Reporter #1: Babe, how do you feel about the Olympics?

Babe: Great. I'm going to win on Sunday, and set world records.

Narrator 1: Several reporters bombarded Babe with questions, talking all at once. Finally, one reporter spoke loud enough to be heard among them all.

Reporter #2: What are you looking forward to the most?

Babe: Winning, what else?

Narrator 2: All the reporters laughed. Babe became famous during her stay in L.A. Movie stars wanted to meet Babe too. Clark Gable was among the movie stars she met.

Clark: Had enough of L.A. yet?

Babe: Well, I haven't been roped into making any movies—yet.

Clark: Funny. I think you have your hands full trying to win, what was it? A gold medal or something?

Babe: A gold medal. Are you implying I might win only one?

Clark: No, of course not. I wouldn't make such an accusation.

Babe: Good. You just stick to making movies. I liked the one you did last year.

Clark: Which? I made around nine movies last year.

Babe: Is that all? You are falling behind! I liked a *Free Soul*.

Clark: Figures you would.

Narrator 2: Before she knew it, the 1932 Olympics came and went. Babe flew back to Dallas, Texas, to celebrate with her family.

Babe: Mom, Dad, I won.

Narrator 1: Babe proudly held up her two gold medals and one silver.

Mom: I'm so proud of you!

Babe: I also set the world records in two events. I did the 80-meter hurdles in 11.7 seconds. Then, I threw the javelin 143 feet and 4 inches.

Dad: A gold medal for each!

Babe: I also competed in the high jump. It was down to me and Jean Shiley.

Mom: She was also on the U.S. team, right?

Babe: Yep. But they disqualified me and claimed I dived, which I didn't. They just gave me a silver medal. But all the reporters took my side. I would have competed in even more events, but I found out the Olympics only allows people to enter three events.

Dad: So, I guess you're making the sports page after all?

Babe: I'm not done yet. I'm thinking of trying my hand at the game of golf.

Epilogue

Narrator 1: Babe went on to pursue a career in golf. She practiced sixteen hours a day.

Narrator 2: In 1938, she married George Zaharias.

Narrator 1: In 1946, she won the U.S. Women's Amateur Tournament and then went on to win seventeen amateur tournaments in a row.

Narrator 2: Babe was frustrated with the lack of professional opportunities for women in sports. She founded the Ladies Professional Golf Association to sponsor more tournaments for women.

Narrator 1: In 1950, Babe was diagnosed with cancer, and it became a fight she was determined to win.

Narrator 2: She went through an operation, and continued on to win the 1954 U.S. Open.

Narrator 1: In 1956, Babe was unable to win the fight against this disease. She remains a symbol of what women can do in the world of sports.

FOLLOW-UP ACTIVITIES

Students may engage in improvisational theatre activities on the theme of sports. For example, the movement activity sculptures can be used. In Chapter Two, this activity is described in greater detail.

Divide students into groups of four. Two students are sculptors and two are "clay." The two sculptors choose a scene from sports to mold the clay into. For instance, they can create the two students who are clay to resemble two people playing tennis, two people shooting baskets, or one person pitching a baseball to the other.

Another extension of this game is for students to create their sculptor scenes like photographs. Assign each group a number. When you say "one," group one quickly assembles their scene. When you say "two," then group two quickly creates their scene, as group one sits down and watches. Continue this until all groups have presented their scenes.

REFERENCES

Freedman, Russell. *Babe Didrikson Zaharias: The Making of a Champion*. New York: Clarion Books, 1999.

Knudson, R.R. *Babe Didrikson Athlete of the Century*. New York: Viking Kestrel, 1985.

Krull, Kathleen, and Kathryn Hewitt. *Lives of the Athletes*. New York: Harcourt Brace, 1997.

Conclusion

I hope you find this book to be useful to you and your students. These scripts offer an opportunity to explore women who contributed to the history of the United States. In so many different fields—medicine, journalism, aviation, and more—these women paved the path for many more to follow in their footsteps.

By integrating the arts into your curriculum, their stories come to life in your classroom. The women in this book represent only a portion of those who changed history. The scripts may be a starting point to explore, understand, and honor the women who played such a valuable role in the shaping of America.

General References

Ashby, Ruth, and Deborah Gore Ohrn. *Herstory: Women Who Changed the World.* New York: Viking Press, 1995.

Keenan, Sheila. *Scholastic Encyclopedia of Women in the United States.* New York: Scholastic, 1996.

McDonough, Yona Zelids. *Sisters in Strength: American Women Who Made a Difference.* New York: Henry Holt, 2000.

Index

About the Author

Chari Smith encourages creativity in children through music and theatre and believes the performing arts are a powerful educational tool. She is the author of *Little Plays for Little People* (Libraries Unlimited/Teacher Ideas Press, 1996) and self-produced the musical story *The Legend of the Boogieman*.

During her career, Chari has worked in education at multiple levels including as a teacher, outreach coordinator, trainer, and researcher. As the outreach coordinator for the Boulder Arts Academy, she directed the performing arts programs Arts Alive!, KinderArts, and Arts on Stage. She also produced two original musicals: *Peter and the Wolf: The Movie that Never Happened* and *All About Opera*. As a teacher, she taught theatre and jazz piano to children of all ages. Chari has also conducted workshops for teachers on how to bring theatre into their classrooms.

Chari attended Berklee College of Music and graduated with honors from Northeastern University with a B.S. in psychology and a minor in music. She continued her education and earned an M.S. in marketing from Golden Gate University. She currently works in education research in Portland, Oregon.